PRAISE FOR

GREAT MONDAYS

Josh gets it! In the volatile, uncertain, complex, and ambiguous world we live in, a company's culture is the only sustainable competitive advantage they have. *Great Mondays* provides anyone—from CEO to frontline associate—a playbook on how to maintain, grow, and evolve a healthy company culture. From personal stories to case studies, Josh illustrates that conversations around culture can be fun and inspiring. If you want to understand more of what culture is and what you can do to help your own company's culture, read this book.

JIM WHITEHURST
President and CEO, Red Hat,
Author of *The Open Organization*

When your culture is off, it can feel amorphous and unmanageable, no matter how bad you want it to change. Josh has changed stagnant cultures into dynamic, healthy, blossoming ones, and now you can too by taking on his designer's mindset. I know, because he helped us to do it.

BRANDON SCHAUER
Head of Enterprise Design, Capital One

As more and more organizations take a DIY approach to culture, they quickly discover how elusive and challenging it can be. *Great Mondays* is every organization's guide to get started with a thorough and simple approach to building their own great culture.

SUNNY GROSSO
Culture Chief, Delivering Happiness

Reporting from the high seas of management consulting, Levine shows why "culture is the keel of business." He generously shares his insights, case studies, and workshop exercises with employers eager to turn reluctant conscripts into motivated volunteers. A must-read for progressive leaders.

MARTY NEUMEIER
Author of *The Brand Gap*, *The Brand Flip*, and *Zag*

The six components of culture outlined in *Great Mondays* is a powerful tool for both start-ups and established companies to intentionally move from a default culture to an incredibly thoughtfully designed one that will attract and retain the best talent.

JENNY SAUER-KLEIN
Founder, The Culture Conference

There is no question that organizational culture is the secret sauce to the success of any organization. It is not a nice-to-have, but a critical business imperative. Josh thoughtfully provides a framework with stories and tactical ideas that can help transform any organizational culture into a high performing one that helps the organization and employee thrive together.

RYAN PICARELLA
President, WELCOA (Wellness Council of America)

Great Mondays is a must-read book for anyone who is trying to foster the right culture within their organization. Having worked with Josh Levine for many years, I find his insight honest and his ideas challenging. Two things that always push me and my business on further.

MATT MANNERS
CEO and Founder, The Employee Engagement Awards

Developing and implementing a positive workplace culture is the central task for everyone in any organization, whether you're a Fortune 500 company or a small volunteer organization. Using fascinating examples and effective templates, Josh Levine guides you toward building a cultures- and values-based workplace.

ANDY DONG
Chair, MBA in Design Strategy at
California College of the Arts

I pulled up my copy of Josh Levine's new book *Great Mondays* on a Monday morning and it made my day. Josh speaks with an authoritative voice honed by years of serious work with culture leaders. He weaves together resonant strands of thought leadership with practical exercises to create organizational culture designs that people will appreciate any day of the week. If you care about company culture, this book is indispensable.

DOUG KIRKPATRICK
Author of *Beyond Empowerment* and
From Hierarchy to High Performance

Investing in your company goes beyond capital expenditures, strategy, even what you're willing to pay for top talent. The companies that win today are those that invest money back into the culture and in their employees. Josh offers you a playbook to map out a workplace culture that doesn't rely on culture tricks. Instead, be ready for a hands-on guide to create a workplace where people want to be. With *Great Mondays*, you will find ways to win the heads, hearts, and hands of your current and future workforce.

SHAWN MURPHY
Author of *The Optimistic Workplace* and *Work Tribes*

Building a great culture is easier said than done, but *Great Mondays* finally shows us how. Josh Levine's style is as informative as it is delightful in this digestible and actionable "how to" on company culture. From small business owners to line managers to executives, this book is for anyone who cares about their culture and wants to do something to make it better.

LAURA PUTNAM
Author of *Workplace Wellness That Works*,
Founder of Motion Infusion

A must-read for HR leaders, culture champions, and anyone looking to attract, retain, and engage the next generation of talent.

ADAM SMILEY POSWOLSKY
Author of *The Quarter-Life Breakthrough*

Culture is not a byproduct of your work; it is your work. Through compelling stories, visual tools, and quick-start guides, *Great Mondays* helps all leaders design more generative, resilient, and rewarding work environments.

LISA KAY SOLOMON
Chair of Transformational Practices and Leadership, Singularity University, and Coauthor of *Design a Better Business*

In *Great Mondays*, Josh Levine outlines an easy-to-follow, no-nonsense approach to designing an amazing company culture—a topic that is often misunderstood and misrepresented. *Great Mondays* is easy and fun to read, full of great stories, and centered around a simple six-step process that makes transformation feel possible and within reach. Filled with deeply insightful and provocative ideas—"Don't try to win the war for talent," "Communities, not customers [are the future]"—this is a don't-miss book for anyone who wants an organization that will thrive in the marketplace of tomorrow.

JOSH ALLAN DYKSTRA
Author of *Igniting the Invisible Tribe*

Great Mondays has the tools and insights to build a great work environment, and get your employees motivated to come to work every day.

TATYANA MAMUT
GM and Product Executive, Strategic Advisor, and Keynote Speaker

Great Mondays takes the mystery out of culture and gives you simple, practical ideas on how to take your workplace from zero to hero. From debunking the myth that everyone needs a ping-pong table and pizza to tackling the real behaviors that can build or break your momentum, Josh provides real-world tips that any leader can put into action every day.

JAMIE COLVIN
Owner, SimplyConnect Consulting

Culture is as powerful a business differentiator as great marketing and superior products. What Josh has done—in practical and pragmatic terms—is develop a blueprint for any organization to create a compelling and differentiated culture for themselves. Brimming with poignant examples and sublime exercises, don't just read *Great Mondays*, action it!

HILTON BARBOUR
Culture Consultant and Marketing Provocateur,
hiltonbarbour.com

GREAT
MONDAYS

GREAT MONDAYS

HOW TO DESIGN
A COMPANY CULTURE
EMPLOYEES LOVE

Josh Levine

Mc
Graw
Hill
Education

New York Chicago San Francisco Athens London Madrid
Mexico City Milan New Delhi Singapore Sydney Toronto

1 2 3 4 5 6 7 8 9   LCR   23 22 21 20 19 18

ISBN   978-1-260-13234-2
MHID   1-260-13234-X

e-ISBN   978-1-260-13235-9
e-MHID   1-260-13235-8

Library of Congress Cataloging-in-Publication Data

Names: Levine, Joshua, author.
Title: Great Mondays : how to design a company culture employees love / Josh Levine.
Description: 1 Edition. | New York : McGraw-Hill Education, 2018.
Identifiers: LCCN 2018027542| ISBN 9781260132342 (hardback) | ISBN 126013234X
Subjects: LCSH: Work environment. | Corporate culture. | BISAC: BUSINESS & ECONOMICS / Workplace Culture.
Classification: LCC HD7261 .L48 2018 | DDC 658.3/12--dc23 LC record available at https://lccn.loc.gov/2018027542

McGraw-Hill Education books are available at special quantity discounts to use as premiums and sales promotions or for use in corporate training programs. To contact a representative, please visit the Contact Us pages at www.mhprofessional.com.

For my managing partner,
the cofounder of our kids.

CONTENTS

ACKNOWLEDGMENTS

Words can't express the gratitude I have for everyone who supported, contributed, and goaded along the way. I'm going to try, anyhow.

First, to all those who helped Culture LabX evolve from a tiny meetup to an international nonprofit. This includes my intrepid cofounders Alyson Madrigan, Lindsay Wolff-Logsdon, Paula Kuhn, Nick Fassler, and Emily Tsiang. Especially Emily Tsiang. In 2014 she and I developed the Culture Code, the unknowing prototype of this book. A special shout-out as well to my ex-coauthor, one-time CLxNYC lab lead, and enduring business luminary Mollie West Duffy; she helped shape the vision for the book and secure the majority of the stories that I've included.

Speaking of stories, thanks to the people who shared their culture tales: Dave Gray, Lauren Cohen, Maggie Spicer, David Kahn, Kate Earle, Dave Kim, Dayla Keller, Jen Dennard, Jessica Fan, Aaron Gibralter, Kristi Riordan, Melanie Duppins, Matt Hoffman, Steve Daniels, Victoria Mitchell, Brandon Schauer, Rikki Goldenberg, Chris Hollindale, Jason Wisdom, Greg Lull and all my friends at Delivering Happiness—Kelsey Wong, Sunny Grosso, and Christine Lai.

A special shout-out to the unstoppable, unflappable Randy Peyser of Author One Stop. Randy would not rest until she found the best home for my book. And in McGraw-Hill Education did she ever. It was there my editor-to-be Noah Schwartzberg saw the possibility in *Great Mondays* and editorial director Donya Dickerson granted me support and patience throughout the process. Thanks to you both.

A few words for the characters I work with: my company's mistress of messaging and my personal pocket pessimist Erica Frye; Shelby Jones for her design insight and Millennial might; and for one of my oldest friends, Lev, who helped me keep things in perspective with gems like "Do you want it perfect or do you want it published?" Good point, Lev.

My mentor, inspiration, and business dad, Marty Neumeier, gets his own paragraph of gratitude. Without Big Mart, I would never have (1) realized business books don't have to be boring, (2) wanted to write one myself, and (3) discovered I could. Thanks, M.

Finally, gratitude to my family. To my mom, dad, and brother for the support and love in this and every one of my previous anxiety-producing endeavors. To Lukas, Sadie, and Mia for their unconditional love. And of course, to my very own Mrs. Maisel, Nikki. How you have the tenacity, energy, and love it takes to run a business, raise a family, and partake in a marriage all at the same time, all with style, I hope to learn someday. No matter where it comes from, I'm just glad it does.

GREAT
MONDAYS

I think most of us are looking for a calling, not a job. Most of us, like the assembly-line worker, have jobs that are too small for our spirit. Jobs are not big enough for people.

—**Studs Terkel**

INTRODUCTION

In 1932, Ed's father lost a finger in a gruesome accident at the factory. Ed was 10. He had watched his father and uncle make mattresses at their shop in the Bronx all his life. As first-generation immigrants they were lucky. Lucky to have their own business. Lucky to be able to support their families. Lucky the Great Depression never took the factory.

After the accident they stopped manufacturing and started selling furnishings. Rockers, tables, dinette sets. Ed came of age during a time of uncertainty and transition. For him stability was a luxury. He studied accounting at the City College of New York near his home. He eventually got a job in the field when he graduated. It was a step up from retail. But when his father got cancer Ed had to step back to run the store. In his mind, Ed never got to have what he wanted—a job that provided steady work. In Ed's mind, he equated steady work with success.

Ed eventually married and had two sons. Mitch was always going to go into business, but Sam was more interested in music. In the 1950s and 1960s Sam played trumpet at school, guitar in a band, and piano because he could. It all led to one audition senior year of high school. He applied for a spot at the most prestigious music school in the country, Juilliard. And he was accepted. Quite the accomplishment for a kid one generation removed from that factory in the Bronx.

Sam never attended a day of classes. His father was firm: music wouldn't provide stability or money. It just wasn't going to work. As Ed saw it, he wouldn't be successful. So, Sam became an accountant.

I grew up with this story. It became Levine family folklore and to this day it colors my view of the world. Maybe back then it wasn't realistic for my dad to have gone to Juilliard, but I've always wondered if he would've been happier pursuing music.

Unlike his own father, my dad encouraged me to seek out work I loved. No longer fearful of the Great Depression or injury from hard labor, he saw meaningful work as part of the new definition of success. By the time I started working, so much had changed from when my dad was diverted from Juilliard. Everything was different—just as my dad's time had been different from his father's. Today work is transforming again. Success is no longer just about making money, today it's about finding meaning.

SUCCESS IS MORE THAN A PAYCHECK

Can anyone actually *love* what they do for work? It may seem naive, but I believe they can. Not only *can* people be passionate about what they do professionally, but *should* find work into which they can throw themselves. It's astounding but true: the average American spends more waking hours per year with coworkers than with family. If we are going to be at work the majority of our lives it better be doing something we love.

We are in an economy that no longer requires a person to take a 40- to 60-hour-a-week office job to make a living wage.

The Web bolsters part-time and work-from-home roles; remote assistants can be hired from anywhere; and anyone can advertise their skills to the world thanks to sites like LinkedIn or YouTube.

Technology has expanded the number and types of opportunities across classes. Sharing economy platforms like Thumbtack and Instacart give hour-at-a-time flexibility to anyone between jobs, shifts, or gigs.

These may or may not be dream jobs, but they do fill the role of getting cash in hand. This makes it all the more feasible to keep searching the market (and our souls) for what it is we really want to do.

I'm not saying that if you find a job you love, it will always be fun or easy. Far from it. Digging into meaningful work requires dedication. But that effort is what makes it all the more rewarding. It's how I believe success should be defined today.

WHY CULTURE MATTERS

What does all this have to do with company culture? Living in a world where job choice is vast and growing means that organizations who want to find and keep great workers better think about what they provide beyond just a paycheck. Even beyond recruiting and retention, it's been shown that businesses get as much in return from a well-designed culture as the employee does.

Workplace culture is one of the single biggest contributors to a company's financial performance. Since 2009, organizations listed on *Forbes*'s "Best Places to Work" list did better than the Standard & Poor's 500 by 84 percent, and since 1998 earned almost three times the cumulative stock market return of the FTSE Russell 2000 and Russell 1000. On the flipside, the 30 lowest-rated public companies on Glassdoor.com underperformed the market by nearly 75 percent.[1]

Culture is the foundation that can support or undermine an employee's behaviors and choices.

For better and for worse, factors like engagement, adaptability, and length of tenure are all influenced by culture. In 2008, when I first realized that there was a tool—poorly understood but with huge potential—that could help businesses improve work lives, it grabbed my head, my heart, and my gut, and it hasn't let go.

FAIL, FAIL AGAIN

By January 2008, I thought I'd have a job. I had left the brand strategy firm where I had worked for almost all 10 of my early career years. I had good recommendations, a large network, and plenty of hope. Then the economy crumbled under the weight of too many subprime mortgages and bad debts. Not one of my job leads held up. Married and with a young son, I had to figure out who I knew and what I could sell them— and quick.

I started consulting in brand strategy while looking for more permanent work. I can't pinpoint the moment it happened, but my job search became a soul search. If I didn't have a job posting to conform to, what did I really want to do with my life? Searching back through clients and projects on which I had cut my teeth, I found that the most interesting ones were those that tackled brand from the inside. They seemed to have the biggest impact on the company and the people. I didn't realize it at the time, but that was when culture design arrived at my door.

I started reading every book and blog about culture I could click on. By 2012, I had been sharing my ideas with anyone who would listen; at parties, networking events, conferences. Not many people understood what I meant. ("Culture? Like ballet or the opera?") Indignant and undeterred, I kept at it.

Then on a chilly night in San Francisco's Mission district, after moderating a spirited panel on work perks, I was accosted by three enthusiastic designers who attended the talk and seemed just as excited about company culture as I was. Did I want to get together for drinks and talk? Definitely! Finally, I had found my people.

It didn't take long for this small group of design-minded professionals to start meeting regularly for beers and culture chat. We never intended for it to be more than a local meetup, but what we would eventually call Culture LabX grew into events and workshops that would start spreading to other cities.

Through this new community we started thinking through some of the most important questions at the time. Beyond trying to define culture, we wanted to understand what made it tick; how we might comprehend it by taking it apart. It was this thread that lead us to the creation of the first version of The Culture Code, the precursor to this book.

I can't claim credit for a lot of the ideas that were in the Culture Code pamphlet. They weren't new. Some we borrowed from business consulting, some from the practices of learning and development professionals in our community, and some came straight from the genius of my original Culture LabX cofounders (without whom this book most definitely wouldn't exist). What was novel about The Culture Code we learned, was assembling these ideas into an interconnected system that could help anyone begin to change how he or she worked.

Over the years we shared it with the Culture LabX community—asking for feedback, welcoming challenges, collecting stories. The more we sent it around the more we saw it resonate with people. From founders of tech start-ups to learning and development professionals, and from traditional enterprises to executives within multinationals, nearly everyone sparked to the ideas we were sharing. The framework was so useful that I began to use it with clients at my agency, also called Great Mondays.

Most of the companies I work with on culture projects come looking for help with *values*, one of the six components. I respond, "Great. Do you know about the rest of culture?" I explain, culture is not just values, it's a whole system. Through the work that was started at Culture LabX, I've helped human resources execs and founders alike see the bigger picture. I help them understand how far it reaches, how they can direct their culture, and how a well-designed culture can make better business decisions.

Since its inception, I have shared and applied the components with many companies, including Humana, Toyota

Innovations, Wellness Council of America, Red Hat, and Credit Karma. Now I teach the framework to my business students so that the next generation of leaders can start their careers with the crucial understanding that culture is a system that can be designed.

A BOOK, A MANIFESTO, AND A GUIDE

I love books. I collect them like idea trophies. The problem for me with this particularly passive medium, specifically those in the business category, is that I don't remember most of what I read. For each book, maybe two key concepts will make their way into my long-term memory for use at a later date. It might be my learning disability, but I'm guessing it's probably the same for many readers.

My goal with this book is not only to improve the number of concepts you'll remember, but to put in your hands a kit of tools that can be used many different ways. Of course, *Great Mondays* can be read page by page, front to back, but it can also be kept on desks as a culture handbook, shared with colleagues as a resource, and opened to any page as a source of inspiration. I wrote this to be more than a book—it's a manifesto, a workbook, and a community-building guide. I wrote this to foment the kind of change that I believe business needs.

NO, REALLY. WHAT'S IN IT?

Great Mondays lays out the six key components of company culture—*Purpose, Values, Behaviors, Recognition, Rituals,*

Cues—illustrating their connection to one another and explaining how they drive an organization's success and its ability to find, keep, and support the best employees. This framework gives readers the tools they can use to increase retention, support employee engagement, and drive business performance, regardless of industry or business size.

I introduce one component in each chapter and unpack what makes it work and how it connects to the rest of the system. Case studies add color and depth to the theories with stories of culture in action from across the extended Culture LabX community.

These accounts are taken from many kinds of organizations, from high-growth Silicon Valley start-ups to nonprofits, universities, and corporations. Some you've heard of, but unlike most business books, the majority are less well-known to mainstream business communities. Why? In my search for contemporary case studies, I purposefully sought out the most relevant stories that hadn't yet been told.

Because no single organization has designed the perfect culture (spoiler: no one ever will), I've assembled the best examples of each component I could find. Each is written to help you imagine how your organization might be just as successful designing and implementing something similar. Or vastly different.

I end each chapter with an exercise or two to help you apply the concepts in your work for your company. While you can fill in the worksheets on your own, they are intended to be developed with culture coconspirators from throughout your organization. It takes time to find the right people and get them to agree to spend a few hours of their afternoon with you. But that's the point: culture design isn't easy because it requires working with others to not only answer the questions, but to put them into action. I want *Great Mondays* to be the stimulant that helps you build your culture team for the short term and the long run.

WHAT IS SUCCESS?

How we spend our days is how we spend our lives. It's easy to get caught up in capitalism's promise of bigger TVs and fancy dinners, but professional success is no longer a gold watch on the day we retire. (There's no watch, and increasingly there's not much retirement, either.) Today work should be much more than a means to an end. We owe it to our families, and ourselves, to love what we do.

Great company culture enables employees to feel seen and supported. It empowers them to bring their whole selves to work and make choices that will help them grow professionally. Undistracted and unmitigated they will be more energized, more creative, more committed, and more productive. That's not just great for our colleagues, it's great for our businesses and our bottom lines.

Whether company president, small-team lead, or corporate wellness manager, *Great Mondays* shares the concepts and tools to help every leader accelerate the next great shift in business. When an organization creates a place where people are inspired and interested, then everyone wins.

What is professional success these days? It's finding a more meaningful life through work. And if we can do that, we might end up loving what we do.

If you want to build a ship,
don't drum up the men to
gather wood, divide the
work, and give orders.
Instead, teach them to yearn
for the vast and endless sea.

—Antoine de Saint-Exupéry

CHAPTER 1

More Than Ping-Pong and Pizza

N SFW activities,[1] absentee management,[2] outright racism.[3] The steady stream of reputation-killing misbehavior continues to dominate news feeds. Reports like these are finally turning more than stomachs as business leaders realize the new truth of twenty-first-century capitalism: ignore company culture at your own risk.

Mitigating risk is far from the only reason to embrace culture as a business tool. Some of today's best-performing companies regularly featured on *Fortune*'s annual list of the "100 Best Companies to Work For"[4] point to *culture* as a major part of their success. Intuit, Autodesk, and Adobe regularly credit culture for inspiring their steady tech stock climbs.

Culture can reverse trends in low-morale, low-satisfaction industries, like it has done for T-Mobile, Delta, and Kimpton Hotels & Restaurants. Working in finance doesn't have to be soul-crushing if there's a great work-life environment like the ones at USAA and Capital One. Even selling commodity goods can be a winning strategy with culture-driven customer service—just look at The Container Store's premium pricing and Build-A-Bear Workshop's plush profits.

Even outside of being a great place to work, the signs that investing in people will bring big benefits to the bottom line are piling up. I was fortunate enough to be at The Culture Summit in San Francisco where Maia Josebachvili, VP of marketing and strategy at Greenhouse Software, preached the concept of lifetime employee value. Using a financial model, she demonstrated how even small gains in onboarding speed increased productivity, and length of tenure can drastically improve a company's returns on their investment in people.[5]

Culture's influence is undeniable. It can be a critical liability that can derail business in a single tweet, or it can be a valuable asset that lifts a middling company to new heights. Culture is the difference between the viable and the vibrant. A business can have shelves of products that fill many holes in the market, maybe even savvy marketing and ads, but without a well-designed culture the company just won't win the hearts and minds it needs to become a long-term industry leader. It's true that only the worst of bad cultures will likely lead to bankruptcy, but for companies with less than stellar cultures, success will always be just out of reach as strategies fail to take hold. To many, floundering is a fate worse than death. First things first, though. Before we can talk about end-runs around the corporate grim reaper, let's define what culture is.

THE GAP BETWEEN WHAT IT IS
AND WHAT TO DO

You know it when you see it. That's what most people might say about the culture at their company. What they really mean is you know when you see its *symptoms*. You may hear it referred to as "climate." Whatever you call it, it's everything from the way emails are written to how work spaces are designed. Does your company have free lunches or casual Fridays? What are its hiring practices? How are employee reviews conducted? All of these are the result of culture. Defining culture as events, moments, and practices provides a sense of what it is, but like describing your first love by listing the items of clothing he or she wore, it falls woefully short of getting to the heart of the matter.

Company culture effects so many things, which makes it notoriously difficult to define. The layman's definition is usually something like: "How we do things around here" or "our behaviors and norms." Management guru Ed Schein sounds like Darwin when he describes culture as "a pattern of shared basic assumptions that was learned by a group as it solved its problems of external adaption and internal integration."[6] I define it as the cause and effect of every choice we make.

These descriptions all have their strengths. The layman's version is easy to understand. Ed's view is interesting. I attempt to be holistic with mine. Take your pick. Attempting to pin down one perfect definition is like trying to look at one of those floating dots on the backs of your eyelids: the more you stare at it, the more it moves.

Culture is the cause and effect of every choice we make.

There's a wide gap between knowing what it is and knowing what to do about it. To wield culture as a business tool, we need to understand how it works. Only then can we design plans to influence it. But before we get to the how, let's answer the why.

THE BUSINESS WORLD TURNED UPSIDE DOWN

A lot of people I talk to about culture say that it's the hot new business trend, and that it seems like the topic popped up out of nowhere. It didn't. In the 1990s and 2000s leaders discussed the idea, it was just rare. Back then culture changes, along with large-scale initiatives like corporate reorgs and strategic realignments, were infrequent events. Now hardly a year goes by when a massive internal shift doesn't occur. Culture change is no longer a one-time event, it's a constant. Or at least it should be. The reason? V-U-C-A.

In the years after the Cold War, the world began to change as communication technology became more sophisticated and available. The most important of all these advances, of course, was the Internet. The web changed not only our everyday lives, social interactions, and nearly all the ways in which companies conduct business, it also influenced the ways governments operated in geopolitical conflicts. To keep the advantage in any modern conflict, negotiation, or nation-building, generals realized decisions had to be made in the moment, on-site— not back at headquarters. The command-and-control style of leadership that had been the strength of the American military was no longer effective as many long-held assumptions crumbled. Competing interests within borders fought for their own ideologies and not the country's, enemies were no longer so easy to find on a map, and military targets often overlapped with centers of civilian activity. Military commanders describe this new reality as VUCA: volatile, uncertain, complex, and ambiguous.[7]

It doesn't take a lot of imagination to see that VUCA describes the battlefield of business, too. A quick survey of the past 20 years reveals this new reality and testifies to what our collective anxiety has been telling us. Start-ups rise and fall in a season, and new ideas upend entire industries in the time it takes to tap "I agree" and allow the latest app to access your contacts. The world is speeding up at an exponential rate. But speed is just one variable of the new physics in which we live.

Loyalty Is Dead

In hotbeds of modern capitalism along the East and West Coasts of North America, one of the most shocking signs of change can be found in the plight of the incredible shrinking tenure. In the 1960s and 1970s, lifetime employment was the norm. Corporate warriors of the 1980s and 1990s dedicated decades to a single company. Now employees stick around for an average of just 18 months, 24 months tops. Corporate loyalty and job security now seem like quaint ideas that your great-grandfather once believed in.

Whether it's a message from a headhunter on LinkedIn, or dissatisfaction with the job itself, it's only a matter of time before the temptation to jump ship becomes too much. In the world of tech, there are too many companies willing to pay too much to fill too many roles. For better or worse, it's reality.

If tech behemoths throwing cash and benefits at your employees isn't scary enough, add to leadership anxiety the rise of the free-agent nation. Job sites like Upwork make remote contract work easy to find. On-demand employment, like TaskRabbit and Lyft, provide flexibility and hourly work with the touch of a button. And emerging infrastructure like 5G will make it even easier to work from anywhere and for anyone.

With tech slurping up talent from across regions and the world, what's to keep butts in seats, if heads and hearts can be elsewhere? Even Middle America won't emerge unscathed from the impact of this hurricane of change. Consider yourself warned.

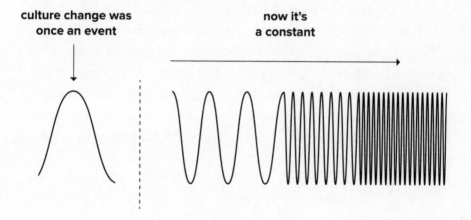

culture change was once an event

now it's a constant

WHO'S THE BOSS

Two of the biggest misconceptions of culture is that (1) company culture is a *thing to be solved* and (2) it's the job of the *leaders*. Let's tackle number one first. Culture isn't a destination or answer to arrive at. It's as alive as the people who live in it, and it's constantly evolving. It requires tending, curation, and updates—call it *continuous improvement* if you want. Would a CFO ever announce that today she solved the company's finances? She would be laughed out of the boardroom. It's as ludicrous to think the VP of human resources would ever say that the company will be focused on culture this quarter and then move on to something else once they'd figured it out.

And number two, the thing about culture being the job of the leaders? While designing and maintaining a great culture will not happen without executive support and modeling, everyone is responsible. Unlike operations or marketing, culture *is* everyone's job. Every choice, action, and conversation affects company culture. When Southwest Airlines' Managing Director of Culture Cheryl Hughey stated, "We all own culture at Southwest" the only thing I could think to say was "Amen, sister."

Be the culture change you want to see in the world.

To succeed, this flip from leader ownership to shared ownership needs to happen inside every employee's skull. If you want something to change in your organization, first ask what shifts you can make that might happily spread to your team. What is your sphere of influence and how can you create the culture you want amongst those people? Almost like Gandhi said: Be the culture change you want to see in the world.

It's always everyone's job. That sounds like a lot of work. And it is. But when an organization gets it right the rewards are immeasurable. More recruiting successes, quicker onboarding, higher engagement, and lower turnover are just a few of the more immediate impacts a well-designed culture can have. Which is why it's worth the effort, and why it's important to have a framework for understanding, designing, and managing your company culture.

The New Rules

Before software began to eat the world, before the great speed-up, and before remote work was the norm, business was easier to predict. Productivity was high, turnover was low, and managers kept employees happy by simply paying more at every annual review. A title bump is on its way if you keep working harder. Back then, the rule of the ladder was simple: climb straight up and you'll succeed. Any other route was perilous. Change of career? Start over. Having a baby? Try again. Spend too much time with family? Do not pass go. This linear thinking was prevalent in the larger market, too.

Back then the enterprise's mantra was "beat the competition by any means necessary," and the equation was simple: advertise more, charge more, sell more, win. And it worked. After all, empires were built on overpriced printer ink.

Fast-forward to today. Hyper-connectivity and hyper-activity mean that an unhappy customer armed with only a YouTube channel and a respectable following can flap his wings in China and cause a PR hurricane in Chicago. In this climate, culture is the only sustainable competitive advantage businesses have. And purposefully designing it is the only way to survive the knockabout, drag-down world of business. From here on out culture rules, and it is *everyone's* job.

Regardless if your title is chief executive officer, senior manager, associate, or contractor, every choice you make affects your organization's culture. Mastery will require not just assigning one person to be responsible for the care and upkeep, but a team dedicated to the task of its support and implementation. Culture isn't a problem to be solved—it's a business function to be supported, evaluated, and applied.

Firms can no longer solely rely on the competitive advantages that are de rigueur in business school. Suing to protect intellectual property? By the time you lawyer up, the next algorithm is already doing it better. Business has changed so radically, even the war for the best and the brightest isn't one you can win—at least not with dollars and donuts.

Culture isn't a problem to be solved; it's a business function to be supported, evaluated, and applied.

Cash ≠ Culture

Go ahead and skip this section if your company's stock is trading above $500. If that's not you, I'm guessing you can't afford to hire Stanford's most recent magna cum laude. In high-demand, low-unemployment economies like Silicon Valley, and more broadly, across the connected world, the tendency has been to throw money at culture problems like talent acquisition and retention. Unfortunately, even free food, fancy facilities, and sky-high salaries can no longer slow turnover. It's an understatement to say that seasoned executives who have long since gotten used to these bribes working are now worried.

Purveyor of corporate reputation Glassdoor reports that culture and leadership are three times more important to employees than salary. Deloitte[8] has shown that over 50 percent of business leaders rate culture, engagement, and retention an urgent issue.

As more work becomes knowledge work, and digital tools enable anyone with a laptop to earn from anywhere, the question every business leader must ask is: "Why work for us?" This question may sound like an existential lament, but it is most definitely a practical query. Top-tier companies, and those that want to be top tier, better have a compelling answer to why anyone would choose to make a home at their organization.

A Sign of the Times

A 2017 *Harvard Business Review* article[9] cites a global survey of factors that contribute to the failure of senior executives who move into new roles. The leading culprit by far is "organizational culture and politics, not lack of competence or managerial skill." This study is emblematic of the change business is facing.

As corporate life cycles and markets accelerate, leaders must grapple with how to create an ecosystem of intrinsically motivated employees who work together for the benefit of the company, their team, and each other. Business leaders now know that they need an outstanding company culture to find, keep, and engage the best employees. What they don't know is *how*.

Design
To conceive or invent. To plan out in systematic, usually graphic form.

Great Mondays provides a framework of six components for those who want to create a sustainable competitive advantage that will equip start-up founders, enterprise managers, and chief executives alike with the tools to address this seismic shift in business. Consider this a guidebook to the system that underlies the single-greatest business advantage to come along since the computer. These tools can be implemented independently to move the culture needle, but together they create the control panel for designing and managing the right culture for their organization: (1) a culture where worker, customer, and company help one another achieve greater success than they ever could achieve alone; and (2) a culture that will propel each toward, and maybe even beyond, their purpose.

THE SIX COMPONENTS OF
COMPANY CULTURE

What will it take to be a place where people not only want to work, but love to work? A *persistent* and *consistent* commitment to designing culture. *Persistent* because culture is a core business capability. If it's simply thought of as this year's priority, it will inevitably be usurped by the next shiny business imperative that comes along. *Consistent* because the best solutions come from constraints. Design is messy. Imagining, creating, and implementing something new is hard, particularly in business. (Just ask any executive who has attempted to build an innovation team.) But by having a consistent system in which to work, the tasks become much more understandable. And doable.

The six-part framework in this book can enable leaders at all levels in all types of organizations to imagine, create, and implement a work-life that supports employees, customers, and businesses. It is a process that builds on its own momentum to become a self-reinforcing system—an upward cycle that will draw in the people who want to help an organization reach its purpose.

The first three components are about creating the vision for the culture, while the second three components are about bringing the culture to life. Together all six components create a system for taking an active role in the outcome of how people feel and are engaged in the organization. It is a system for designing a culture that employees love.

Purpose

WHY AN ORGANIZATION
EXISTS BEYOND MAKING
MONEY.

 *Values*

SHARED BELIEFS ABOUT WHAT
IS MOST IMPORTANT WHEN
CONDUCTING BUSINESS.

 Behaviors

CHOICES MADE BY EMPLOYEES
THAT ARE GUIDED BY PURPOSE
AND VALUES.

 Recognition

PROGRAMS THAT ENCOURAGE
BEHAVIORS THAT BRING THE
CULTURE TO LIFE.

 Rituals

RECURRING GROUP ACTIVITIES
THAT BUILD AND STRENGTHEN
RELATIONSHIPS.

 Cues

REMINDERS THAT HELP
EMPLOYEES AND LEADERS STAY
CONNECTED TO THE FUTURE.

Purpose → Values → Behaviors →

An audacious goal can mobilize large groups of individuals. Whether it's raising money for a school, joining a religious community, or increasing awareness of climate change, if a cause is ambitious enough, it will attract and energize people to join a cause that is greater than themselves. But rallying people toward bold achievements isn't only for nonprofits and spare time. Businesses too need to identify an inspiring reason for being. Writing your purpose statement is the first step in culture design. When a company can identify and articulate a compelling *purpose*, it will attract and energize the talented people who will help take their team and company to the next level.

Values are behavioral guideposts that establish how to act on the way to achieving our purpose. This is the second component of culture design and it should come to life with every decision. A product lead should consider the company's values when evaluating a potential feature. A line manager needs to mentor with values in mind. The head of people operations needs to work with the hiring manager to look for candidates with similar values to the company *and* consider how the entire interview experience itself reflects what the organization believes. Everyone across the organization needs to know the firm's values and how they inform their own responsibilities.

Behavior is the third piece of culture design. Imagine it as the path from where you are today to purpose, guided by the guardrails of values. Behaviors set precedents, ensuring each person understands what is expected when he or she makes choices at work. Together, the first three components provide the trajectory for talent to make better decisions with less oversight. Culture becomes a tool that enables macro- (not micro-) management.

→ **Recognition** → **Rituals** → **Cues** →

Recognition, the fourth component of culture design, is not new, but no less important. When an individual or team can see that the result of their effort is appreciated and how it has contributed to a larger goal, they feel satisfied, and perhaps even motivated to do it again better. Now flip that. Is there anything more frustrating than putting in the time on a project and not seeing results? It's not long until disheartening sentiments, which could be entitled "why did I work so hard on that?" start to flood in.

Not only does engagement suffer from insufficient or ineffective recognition, but it can be a drag on resources and momentum in the form of replacement cost. Companies with high rates of employee recognition have a 31 percent lower voluntary turnover than companies with poor recognition cultures.[10]

Don't be misled, though; handing out coffee cards and plaques alone won't work. There are many opportunities to recognize, and many ways to do it.

Relationships are the synapses of culture; if they aren't strong and abundant behaviors begin to diverge between departments, offices, and roles. *Rituals*, the fourth component of culture design, provide ways for coworkers to build and strengthen relationships at work, inspiring connections across physical and virtual boundaries. Gallup has demonstrated that those who have a best work friend are seven times more likely to stay longer than those without.[11] Not that everyone needs a bestie in the next cubicle over, but the statistic shows the power of relationships. Weekly coffee dates, monthly lunch-and-learns, and annual retreats are just some of the rituals that build and strengthen relationships.

Cues are the verbal and behavioral reminders of the organization's ideal future, and the final component of culture design. The most common example of a cue is the mission statement on the wall, but other tools can also elevate long-term thinking so that the day-to-day activities of work don't obscure the *why* of work. Cues are the connection between tactics and strategy—the end and the beginning of a holistic system that turns work into meaning and hours into purpose.

FROM THE TOP

In the following chapters, I'll take you through each culture component, explaining its role in culture design and its impact on business, adding context and color with stories from organizations who have put it into practice. Let's start at the beginning with purpose.

If we crave some
cosmic purpose, then
let us find ourselves
a worthy goal.

—Carl Sagan

CHAPTER 2

Purpose

Millennials may have put the idea of "meaning at work" on the cover of business magazines, but humanity's search for significance started way before Gen Y was around. Viktor Frankl—neurologist, psychiatrist, and author of *Man's Search for Meaning*—believed that humans are driven by a desire to seek meaning in life. His work in the field, which started in the early twentieth century, is the precursor to many of today's popular psychotherapies. Frankl found that positive life purpose and meaning was associated with five elements: *strong religious beliefs, membership in groups, dedication to a cause, life values, and clear goals*—in other words, believing in and contributing to something bigger than ourselves. From cause-driven fund-raisers to religious practice, there are countless ways in which people find purpose. At the end of the day, no matter what medium we choose, seeking purpose, meaning, and significance is all about answering one question:

Why am I here?

But I've got another question for you:

What's work got to do with humanity's search for meaning?

MEANING BEYOND MONEY

Why work? The reasonable response might once have been "to make money," and for some that's still true. But as our economy has evolved and work options have proliferated, the answer has changed for a growing majority of people—they want more than just a paycheck.

For too long, MBA programs have taught that the primary function of business is to create a profit. That's not enough any longer. Profit is just proof that the work that's been done has value. The more value, the more profit. Any other logic sacrifices the customer for the business.

Purpose
A grand vision of why an organization exists beyond making money.

John Mackey, founder of the now Amazon-owned Whole Foods, once said: "You can't live if you don't eat, but you don't live to eat. And neither does business exist primarily to make a profit. It exists to fulfill its purpose."[1] He believed that it is the company's job to take care of the employees, the employees' job is to take care of the customers, and if you do all that right, then customers would naturally take care of the profit. Short that system and you'll be trading long-term success in pursuit of short-term cash. Bestselling author and business guru Tom Peters underscores this point when he says: "Excellent customer experiences depend *entirely* on excellent employee experiences." If you want to build

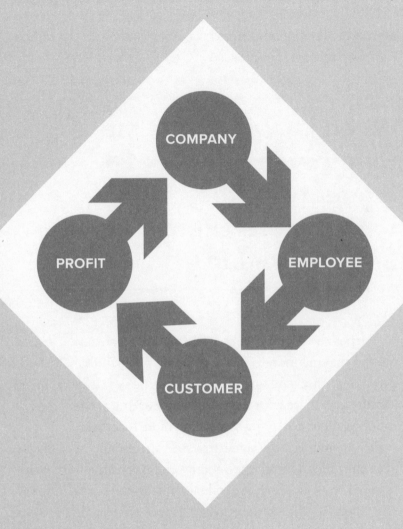

PROFIT IS JUST PROOF.

DON'T SACRIFICE THE CUSTOMER

FOR THE BUSINESS.

a perpetual motion machine of value as Mackey describes, the *only* place to start is purpose.

When individuals come together in pursuit of a bigger goal, they tend to find more energy and motivation.

Purpose is a grand vision of why an organization exists beyond making money; it is a company's North Star. To find, keep, and motivate great talent, businesses leaders must identify and share with the world why working at their organization is about achieving something more together.

When individuals come together in pursuit of a bigger goal, they tend to find more energy and motivation—they are inspired to work. Each individual contributor has a different role, likely in different locations. Purpose enables them to see how their work helps move the team towards their goal. Purpose creates community and inspires responsibility. Purpose is the great unifier, bringing together motivations, people, and goals.

When demand for employees outruns supply, anything short of a Google-sized offer will be discarded into the "maybe" category. Today businesses don't just compete for customers, they compete for talent. Leaders who still believe that people are willing to trade their time for only a paystub lose.

Paychecks sit at the bottom of a business interpretation of Abraham Maslow's classic hierarchy of needs; it is a basic necessity that can be fulfilled in many ways. Purpose, on the other hand, rises to the top. In an evolved society like ours, which company do you think will attract the best people: the one that inspires, giving its employees a chance to achieve something greater, or the one that's simply about turning a profit? If you are looking to hire, retain, and keep engaged a skilled workforce, these days it's going to take more than cash; it's going to take purpose.

THE PROBLEM GETTING TO PURPOSE

Why don't more companies get clear about why they are in business? Because of the nearly inescapable gravity of traditional economic theory. Mackey's quote about purpose was uttered in response to the conservative economist and Nobel Laureate Milton Friedman. "There is one and only one social responsibility of business—to use its resources and engage in activities designed to increase its profits so long as it stays within the rules of the game."[2] Friedman espoused this in 1970. Unfortunately, many traditional business leaders still think this way, and it's easy to see how there is no role for purpose in this ancient worldview. Don't fall for it. Companies who short the circuitry of modern business by skipping the employee are doomed to customer backlash and long-term failure.

An Unshakeable Belief

The Bill & Melinda Gates Foundation's work is guided by the belief that every life has equal value. Whether it's sparking a global movement to eradicate polio, inventing and delivering new vaccines, or ensuring that people who live on less than $2 a day have the right set of digital financial solutions, the people who show up to work at the Gates Foundation focus their work on the areas around the world that have the greatest need.

"I see our purpose best when I look at my colleagues and partners," says program officer Dave Kim. His team, Financial Services for the Poor, works on technologies that provide economic solutions to the world's neediest populations. He says while walking the halls he will catch a conversation about the latest effort to combine the best of human-centered design with data science to reimagine the role of mobile money agents in East Africa. "Next door," he reports, "you'll hear about the latest efforts to rally the global scientific community around developing new platforms to accelerate contraceptive drug discovery."

While the topics are wide-ranging, the common thread across all their work, says Dave, is the focus on impact, and the unshakeable belief that a more just world is long overdue.

I can imagine when trying to crack a problem as big and seemingly ever-present like poverty, it can be easy to lose your bearings. But Dave and his colleagues see their purpose as a resource that keeps them driven. "It is faith in our work and . . . belief in the people who actively seek to make tomorrow's promise today's reality that feed our impatient optimism and bring us back into the office each morning."

GOOD PURPOSE STATEMENTS

To help people be their best
financial selves.
CREDIT KARMA

To create a world where anyone can get work,
wherever and whenever they want.
SNAG

To bring inspiration and innovation to every athlete*
in the world. *If you have a body, you are an athlete.
NIKE

To inspire and nurture the human spirit—one person,
one cup, and one neighborhood at a time.
STARBUCKS

To create a better everyday life
for the many people.
IKEA

To nourish families so they can
flourish and thrive.
KELLOGG'S

I hear you. Of course, a social-minded organization funded by one of the world's wealthiest families would have to have a compelling purpose. But the truth is that while the Gates Foundation might be able to define their purpose more easily than most, every organization out there has a purpose to discover. Or rediscover.

Recalibrating Your Culture

Digital consultancy Adaptive Path was founded in 2001 on the idea that the Internet could be much more valuable to business and the world if websites were designed with the user in mind. If only companies would invest in this new idea called "user experience." Adaptive Path's purpose was to improve the usefulness of the web by being the champions of User Experience Design (UX in designer speak). And after a decade of blog posts, keynotes, and groundbreaking work they succeeded. Today, UX Design is a skill every company's digital team has.

The problem for the team at Adaptive Path was that the more UX Design was understood, the less important the company's place in the world became. While reaching their purpose, they had lost their way.

They continued to do award-winning work for clients like NPR, *Harvard Business Review*, Twitter, and Airbnb, but their team of first-rate consultants were no longer first-rate motivated. Without an inspiring purpose to fulfill, they didn't know why they were there. Leadership saw that the company needed to rediscover their answer to "Why work?" or they would soon see their talent, focus, and profits wane.

A NOTE ON MISSION AND VISION

Mission statements clarify what an organization does, for whom they do it, and how. Vision statements describe a concrete image of what achieving that mission will look like. If done well they can be useful business tools. Do you really need a purpose statement, too? In a world of increasing transparency and shortening distances between company and customer, these statements miss the most important why: what benefit the company creates for current and future customers, the communities in which they operate, and the world. Purpose statements guide, inspire, and rally customers and employees to join a cause greater than themselves. A great purpose statement is a company's North Star.

I was fortunate enough to have been asked by Adaptive Path's CEO Brandon Schauer to help rediscover their purpose. With seven cofounders and a kettle of profoundly smart employees, getting everyone to agree on a single purpose wasn't easy.

At first the process of rediscovering their purpose felt like navel-gazing, Brandon reflects. "But, we took a long listen to what our employees, leaders, and customers all felt most deeply about. And we looked at what we uniquely did." They brought the right people into the process and prototyped through many rounds and workshops to uncover this new vision of the future. Gradually their renewed sense of purpose emerged.

Purpose statements guide, inspire, and rally customers and employees to join a cause greater than themselves.

Although Adaptive Path still created beautiful digital properties, they realized that wasn't their purpose. They existed to create great *human experiences*, regardless of how. This new aspiration applied to everything they did: training and workshops, conferences and writing, and of course, consulting for major businesses.

The process of rediscovering their purpose was essentially editing down to their core and then amplifying what they found. It came from the work they had always done and the ideas they had always shared. In those first 10 years it was too big of an idea for them to see, but now it was the right size and the right time. Their new purpose was grand enough to lead Adaptive Path through their next decade.

Once their purpose became clear, every tough decision became more obvious, the right paths became clear, and it became evident how they should do things, as a brand, and as individuals.

Their new North Star helped them grow audiences, seek work that had impact, and ultimately join a bigger organization with a purpose aligned with their own. They agreed to be acquired by Capital One just a few years after.

ANSWERING THE BIG QUESTIONS

Convinced purpose is important? You aren't home free yet. During the decade that I've been doing this work, I've found that the biggest challenge nearly every executive team must face is *internal*—their inability to let go of the most immediate and pressing parts of the business. I get it. Rolling out the new product update and hitting quarterly financial goals are important. It can be scary to put that work down for even a day. But finding a company's purpose isn't about this quarter, or even this year; it requires taking the long view.

Imagining what doesn't exist is hard, but that's exactly what you must do to discover your purpose because it's your future. How might the world be different (in a good way) because of your company? Step back and ask your team, why does your company matter? Why will it be remembered?

I'm not asking for realism—that we get enough of. Think big. In attempting this work, my advice is to not get bogged down in the specifics. Go far, as fast as possible. To find your purpose you need to pass it first. Go 25, 50, 100 years in the future with your ideas. Don't worry, you can always reel it back in.

Think you can't do it? I disagree. At the end of this chapter I've provided everything you need to get started. The exercise and examples have helped many leadership teams stretch their brains in the right direction, and I'm certain it can help you, too.

Communicating and Implementing

Purpose answers the question "Why work?" Purpose guides employees and the choices they make. But like strategy without action, purpose statements need to be applied to be meaningful. Purpose statements are great for inspiring, but it is leadership's job to ensure everyone knows how to connect it to the company's day-to-day operations. That's what Chapter 4, Behaviors, is all about; it discusses how leaders use purpose and values to establish behaviors, the symptom of culture.

What is your organization's reason for being? Finding your company's purpose isn't going to make work easier, but it will provide more clarity to help leaders make hard decisions, more meaning to help employees do their jobs with more energy, and more value to help customers choose your brand more often.

Purpose Quick-Start

Uncover your company's purpose by defining why it should be remembered.

WHY ARE YOU IN BUSINESS?

Write Your Company's Obituary

Of all the tools I've used with clients throughout the years, this exercise is the one that gets the most mileage by far. Why write an obituary for your organization? By imagining the organization as dead, executives, who are usually consumed with the details, get permission to let go of the minutia. With day-to-day concerns out of the way leaders have room to think bigger.

Here's the overview: it is 25 years from now and the company has ceased to operate. It is your job to describe why the company will be remembered in three to five short paragraphs. When complete, the obituary should answer the questions: What were the company's greatest accomplishments, and how did it change the world?

We usually work with executives and vice presidents, but you can involve a diversity of roles depending on who needs to be brought into the process. Include those who know the company well (veterans), those who have a knack for seeing the future (visionaries), and those who might be challenging to get on board later if they are left out (blockers).

WHY YOU'RE DOING THIS
To answer the question "Why are we in business beyond making money?"

HOW YOU'LL DO IT
A half-day workshop.

WHO SHOULD PARTICIPATE
8 to 12 colleagues including veterans, visionaries, and blockers.

WHERE IT SHOULD HAPPEN
A large room with lots of wall space and room to collaborate.

WHAT YOU'LL NEED
A poster-sized sticky pad, lots of markers, dot stickers, a copy of the worksheet and a half-day of uninterrupted time.

HOW LONG YOU'LL NEED
3 hours.

Download this exercise to work on with your team at **greatmondays.com**

INSTRUCTIONS

1. Split workshop participants into three to four teams. No team should have more than five members.

2. Instruct each team to work together to write the first draft of their obituary. They should end up with three to five short paragraphs that include only the most important details. *Hint: Bulleted lists don't work nearly as well as complete sentences. Don't let anyone go that route. Time:* 30 to 45 minutes

3. Ask each team to make any final edits and then transpose their entire obituary by hand onto the large sticky pad. (Yes, they must write it out. And yes, they must put it up so everyone can see.) *Time:* 30 minutes

4. Invite one person from each team to read back his or her obituary. *Time:* 20 minutes

5. Once all teams have presented, pass out the dot stickers. Each person will place them next to the words and phrases he or she finds the most compelling or relevant. Each person gets six to eight dots and can vote on anything, including his or her own answer. You can even put multiple dots on one idea if it seems particularly important. *Time:* 15 minutes

6. Once everyone has used all their stickers, ask one person to tally up the votes, and mark the words and phrases that were most popular. *Time:* 10 minutes

7. As a group, discuss what you notice and what it might mean for the purpose of the organization. Talk about which got the most votes and why. Look for patterns. Are there any common themes? What stands out? What was expected or unexpected? *Time:* 30 minutes

A good obituary avoids getting dragged down by reality, and instead leans in to the seemingly impossible.

{ obituary example }

Petcha will be missed.

Petcha.com, known the world over as the global brand that created local connections between people and their pets, closed today. The company was built on the premise that pet owners have known for years: take care of your pet and you take care of yourself. The site completely eradicated the need for shelters because every pet that needed to be cared for found an owner who needed that love as well.

The sudden rise in national well-being that occurred in the late 2020s was directly connected to Petcha's success. Petcha reversed the decline in health due to stress and anxiety that most of the working population suffered from. The company's prevalence inspired the creation of the National Wellness index so that other communities could track the benefits of pet ownership. Petcha.com increased Gross National Product *and* Gross National Happiness. It will be missed.

AFTER IT'S GONE, WHY WILL YOUR COMPANY BE REMEMBERED?

Write Your Company's Purpose Statement

Now that the group has surfaced some of the elements of the company's reason to exist, it's time to sharpen the thinking. Using the most important words or phrases from the obituary (which should still be up around the room) as a starting point, draft a purpose statement. It should be written in 25 words or less and start with the phrase "To <action verb>." (*See the list of Good Purpose Statements earlier in the chapter for guidance and inspiration.*)

INSTRUCTIONS

1. Ask each participant to make three attempts at writing a purpose statement.
   Time: 20 minutes

2. Have each person read to the group the one he or she considers the best. Request that someone transcribe each on a large sheet or whiteboard.
   Time: 20 minutes

3. Discuss as a group what works about each, and choose the one that best captures your company's purpose. You might want to combine two if there are elements that work in both. Make any final edits and rewrite for the group to reflect on.
   Time: 20 minutes

{ purpose statement example }

Petcha's Purpose

To help more people have better lives by becoming great pet owners.

WRITE THREE PURPOSE STATEMENTS, EACH 25 WORDS OR LESS.

1. To _____ _____
                \<ACTION VERB\>

_____

_____

_____

_____

2. To _____ _____
                \<ACTION VERB\>

_____

_____

_____

_____

3. To _____ _____
                \<ACTION VERB\>

_____

_____

_____

_____

It's not hard to make
decisions when you
know what your
values are.

—Roy Disney

Values

There are many ways to climb a mountain. Setting a goal to reach the summit can inspire, but the destination alone won't tell you which trail to take. Unfortunately, that's exactly what happens too often in business. When only results are rewarded even the most talented may take the wrong route—shortcuts that undermine larger business objectives. In a well-designed culture, the end should never justify the means.

The peak of any business is purpose, but without guides, it is hard to know which way is best. The path to the top must be defined by an organization's values. When written well, values are shared beliefs about what is most important when conducting business. They guide the choices each person, team, and business unit makes within an organization as they strive to achieve their shared goals. So how does a company decide what its values are? Step one, start with the behaviors you want.

DEFINING VALUES: START HERE

In the early stages of an organization's life, the founders dictate the culture. In most cases nearly every person has some direct contact with his or her company's leaders. At a small scale, proximity to executives supports the spread of behaviors. The founders are the models; the more time an employee spends with them, the more they are emulated. But as organizations grow that direct contact rapidly diminishes, and the organization's behaviors begin to evolve on their own. The culture starts to evolve beyond the founder. It's time to actively choose which behaviors you want.

Values
Shared beliefs about what is most important when conducting business.

Which colleagues embody the best version of the company? These are your Culture All-Stars, and they are shining examples of values brought to life. The ideal high-potential employees are not just rich in skill, but they carry the behaviors that will spur the kind of culture leaders want as the company grows.

Finding employees who represent the ideal culture is what New York–based coding boot camp, The Flatiron School, did when they began to think seriously about their unique culture. But it didn't start that way.

At first, employees were asked to describe the organization's culture in general. Words like kind, smart, fun, hard-working, collaborative, and driven were common. Chief operating officer Kristi Riordan says "that was encouraging, but we thought we could do better [by being] more precise in our definition." Great call, Kristi.

Most organizational values end up being generic because, well, it's easier to get to the obvious ones. But great values come from digging deeper. Successful brands understand that without differentiation they'll wash away in a sea of sameness. The same goes for values. Like great brands, values are best when highly differentiated.

Like great brands, values are best when highly differentiated.

Under Kristi's guidance, they tried again, this time specifically asking for words that describe employees who exemplify the culture. This time she found patterns that revealed values that were unique, compelling, and true: Make no little plans; Radiate positivity; Be scrappy; Pursue mastery; Work together.

Through this process, The Flatiron School discovered that values are as much about the future as they are about today. Kristi observed that their new values "provide us with a reminder of who we are as much as who we want to be as we continue to grow."

NOT JUST A HEADLINE

But don't get it twisted. Even the most unique values will fail to guide behaviors if employees don't know what they mean. Values without definitions are fair game for interpretation. To be effective, every manager, employee, and line leader must know what is behind the phrase, and the actions and behaviors that exemplify that value.

The founders of digital marketing platform Percolate, Noah Brier and James Gross, recognized early in the life of their company the importance of values. They have put a lot of thought and life into their culture, but it is one small piece that has helped elevate their values beyond headlines—each value's description is followed by a question.

For example, the value of "Accelerating" is followed by the question: "Does this decision move us closer to the company's mission and vision?" This question challenges the reader to connect the value to their own choices. The value of "Judge Percolate against

> Culture All-Stars embody the culture for which the company strives. Choose people who are implicit leaders—those colleagues tend to follow, not because of their title or role, but because of who they are.

Percolate" is followed by the question: "Is what I'm doing truly exceptional or am I allowing it to be watered down by outside influences?" The value of "Success is measured in advocates" is followed by the question: "How is what I'm doing helping to drive advocacy?" These interrogations bring the values to life for each employee personally.

These postscripts help employees understand that these values aren't just platitudes, but decision-making tools. (The full list of Percolate's values and some additional thoughts about them are at the end of this chapter.)

Not every company is lucky enough to have leaders with such clarity. Because values are an exercise in prioritization, the biggest challenge most organizations face is deciding which beliefs and behaviors are most important.

They Can't All Be Values

When a belief is codified as a value, it says to everyone: "This. This right here is what's most important." While tempting, you can't claim that every belief is the most important. The more items on the values list, the less important each one becomes, and the less clarity they provide. There's a limit to how many get to be values, and that number is five.

Yes, there are organizations that have a shopping list of values that count into the teens, but in my experience, this is self-defeating because (1) the list gets harder to remember as it grows, and more importantly (2) values exist to help people make choices, particularly difficult ones. When times are tough, values should help clarify hard decisions, which is why what is omitted can be as important as what is included.

LIVE, DON'T LAMINATE

Words on a wall do not a value make. It is the responsibility of business leaders to support everyone in the organization, so they not only understand what each value means, but can put it into action in their own work.

When thinking about how to convert values into actions it's important to understand the role personal values play. Every person has underlying assumptions about the way the world works, and it's from those assumptions that *personal values* spring. If personal and organizational values are similar, or at least not contradictory, an individual will likely be able to make choices that are best for the company.

However, the greater the divide between an individual's values and those of the organization, the harder it will become for that person to make good choices. If the difference between the individual's and the organization's values is too far to bridge, most likely the person just isn't going to thrive there.

But not every value gap is a deal breaker. If team leaders and managers acknowledge that value alignment is important, then it can be a very effective culture-building tool in connecting values to behaviors.

San Francisco experience design firm WHISK started explicitly connecting its values to organizational behavior through a values alignment exercise during an early organizational growth spurt. Founder Maggie Spicer began hosting internal workshops to help each team member map the similarities and differences between WHISK's values and their own core values. "If there were any significant differences, we talked about the implications," she reports.

PERSONAL VERSUS CORPORATE VALUES

Personal values

Words, phrases, and symbols that represent *one individual's beliefs* about what is most important when conducting one's life. They guide the choices that the individual makes as he or she strives to achieve his or her *personal goals*.

Corporate values

Words, phrases, and symbols that represent *shared beliefs* about what is most important when conducting business. They guide the choices that individuals make within an organization as they strive to achieve a set of *shared goals*.

For example, one of WHISK's values is "trust." If there was a gap in which an employee was inherently less trusting, he or she might be more likely to choose to keep a failure to him- or herself. But for the benefit of the business, the best action might be to share it broadly with the team so that everyone can learn from it. Understanding those differences is key to values alignment.

In addition to surfacing differences in values between the individual and the business, the work helped Maggie and her team identify the employees who would collaborate best together and even projects with which their values were aligned. The company has since worked with clients like the San Francisco Opera, Airbnb, and Levi Strauss & Co. in this capacity and to great success.

Seeing the Boundaries of Culture

Values are guideposts. It is a leader's responsibility to uncover where they stand and point out the route most likely to lead to the summit. The values of companies like Percolate, The Flatiron School, and WHISK provide a path that *guides* their employees. But it's important that the path is left wide enough so that each person has the latitude to find his or her own way. The right number of markers permit teams to make their trek together safely, avoiding shortcuts and dangerous passes. But be careful. Too many values leave only a tightly prescribed path, with little room for exploration and discovery.

Shared beliefs inspire the behaviors a company wants, but they should be reassessed every few years. As a company grows, values should be allowed to evolve to reflect the changes and new challenges it faces. Small teams at a young start-up may have no problem sharing ideas when they are all in the same room. But as the company grows and more people are sorted into more departments, an emphasis on collaboration and teamwork might need to be elevated.

When workers, managers, and leaders understand the intent behind their company's values and are aware of how they relate to their own assumptions, values will become a powerful culture design tool, and one that's needed to identify the next component in the system: behaviors.

AIM FOR THREE TO FIVE VALUES

When creating or refreshing your values, cap them at five. It's not an easy number to hit, but the more on the list, the less meaning each value will have, and the less memorable each will be.

Values Quick-Start

Let the people who are the best of your culture help you define your values.

WHO REPRESENTS THE FUTURE OF YOUR CULTURE?

Spot Your Culture All-Stars

A company's values don't emerge fully formed from a founder's or consultant's head. The behaviors they are based on already exist. Your job is not to create them, but simply to find them. Don't get stuck in your own head. Great value-driven behaviors are all around. With a company full of employees, look for the ones you admire. If you find yourself thinking "if only I could get *everyone* to act just a little more like her" you've struck culture gold. Find your Culture All-Stars and you have found those who already know what your company truly values.

WHY YOU'RE DOING THIS
To identify the three to five beliefs your company holds most dear.

HOW YOU'LL DO IT
A half-day workshop.

WHO SHOULD PARTICIPATE
Up to 5 VPs and/or line leaders from across the organization.

WHERE IT SHOULD HAPPEN
A medium-sized room with lots of wall space and room to collaborate.

WHAT YOU'LL NEED
Post-it Notes, markers, and a copy of this exercise for each participant.

HOW LONG YOU'LL NEED
3 hours.

Download this exercise to work on with your team at **greatmondays.com**

INSTRUCTIONS

1. Ask each participant to identify two amazing colleagues—those whom they would consider Culture All-Stars. Think of employees that represent what is good today, and those that exemplify the kind of culture you'd like in the future.
   Time: 15 minutes

2. Instruct each person to list three specific behaviors that exemplify why he or she selected that person. Write each behavior on its own Post-it Note.
   Time: 15 minutes

3. Have each participant present to the group who he or she chose and why.
   Time: 20 minutes

4. After everyone has shared, stick up the Post-it Notes on a worksurface or whiteboard that everyone can see. Group any duplicate behaviors.
   Time: 30 minutes

5. Together, talk about what each behavior might mean to the organization's values. For example, if someone described how they really liked the way Dantell asks people outside her department for feedback before her quarterly sales presentation, you might say you value "employees who get out of their own heads," "cross-department collaboration," or "feedback and prototyping." During the discussion write down the ideas that you find compelling and post them on the wall near the behavior. The more the better.
   Time: 30 minutes

HINT: *Don't try to write short values headlines at this point. Consider these ideas "value themes" to allow room for experimenting and mistakes.*

6. Time for some analysis. Observe which values were repeated or are related. Which value themes feel like they belong together? Sort the notes until they are organized in clusters that makes sense. It's okay if you have more than five groups at this point.
   Time: 30 minutes

7. Which of the themes seem more compelling, true, or urgent than the others? Try to narrow your choices to six or fewer idea clusters. Mark the value themes the majority of your group agrees should be elevated and move the rest to another wall.
   Time: 20 minutes

8. Within each remaining value theme, look for the words or phrases that best capture the entire idea. Move to the top of each grouping one or two notes that can act as a title or write a new one.
   Time: 20 minutes

9. Rewrite these value theme titles on a new sheet. This list is the starting point of your new values.
   Time: 5 minutes

   BONUS: *Once you've completed this exercise, bring in your Culture All-Stars to review what you created. What do they think? Can they spot anything that's missing? What could be removed?*

WHAT'S NEXT

From here it's no small feat to arrive at your company's three to five final values; the key will be prioritizing what is most important. That said, by the end of this exercise you will have most, if not all, of the ingredients you need. The ideas within your value themes are the draft of your description. Write them up into a coherent paragraph that answers the question: "What does this value mean?" The specific behaviors with which you started the exercise should be cited as examples of living the values. Use these to answer the question: "What does this value look like in action?"

What are the one to four words that will be the value's name? Writing pithy, differentiated, and memorable headlines is a job for a pro. Sure the group could come up with something satisfactory but see if you can't find someone from your marketing or brand teams who would be willing to help.

CONGRATULATIONS, YOU ARE ON YOUR WAY TO CREATING YOUR VALUES.

	BEHAVIOR	VALUES THEME
CULTURE ALL-STAR #1	1.	1.
	2.	2.
	3.	3.

	BEHAVIOR	VALUES THEME
CULTURE ALL-STAR #2	1.	1.
	2.	2.
	3.	3.

WHAT GOOD VALUES LOOK LIKE

They're brief.

They should be easy to remember, display, and share.

Keep each value title to between one and four words.

They're well-defined.

Each value must be supported by descriptions of what the

value means, and what employees should do as a result.

They're unique.

It's easy to come up with generic values like "innovative."

Go farther and identify those values that make your

organization special.

They're limited in number.

The more values you have, the less they mean. Keep your

list to five or fewer.

They're actionable

Employees should be able to use the company's values to

make important decisions.

VALUES EXAMPLE 1: THE FLATIRON SCHOOL

HEADLINE	DESCRIPTION	SUBJECT
Make no little plans.	Build for scale; create for the whole world; execute short-term goals in view of long-term strategy.	(Vision)
Radiate positivity.	Be nice; have fun; find what to love about your work and surroundings.	(Attitude)
Be scrappy.	Get things done; be resourceful; embrace change; thrive in moments of ambiguity.	(Execution)
Pursue mastery.	Be a beginner; always be learning; do a lot better; value feedback.	(Performance)
Work together.	Collaborate; listen intently and over-communicate; embrace transparency; empower others to succeed.	(Teamwork)

WHAT I THINK WORKS ABOUT THESE

Unique, check. Five or fewer, check. Brief, check. The Flatiron School has almost nailed all the qualities that make for good values. Bonus points for identifying categories.

WHAT I THINK COULD BE IMPROVED

While each value's definition says what to do ("be nice"), will these help employees make decisions quickly and decisively? Perhaps. I'd like to see them go further with examples of each imperative.

VALUES EXAMPLE 2: PERCOLATE

HEADLINE	DESCRIPTION	QUESTION
Accelerating	A start-up isn't determined by size; it's a company fueled for productivity, speed, and removing friction. We must keep this spirit alive.	Does this decision move us closer to the company's mission and vision?
Thoughtful by design	We aim for thoughtfulness in everything we do. This should be felt by colleagues, customers, and competition.	Will this interaction leave the person on the other end feeling like I care deeply about their time?
Judge Percolate against Percolate	Know that everyone else has a lower bar than we do; never compromise.	Is what I'm doing truly exceptional or am I allowing it to be watered down by outside influences?
Success is measured in advocates	We are truly successful when our customers, employees, and partners become our champions.	How is what I'm doing helping to drive advocacy?
You own this company	As we grow, it is your responsibility to ensure that we're awesome. If it sucks, make it better.	If I were the owner of this company outright, would I still do what I'm doing?
Constant questioning	Asking 'why?' isn't just for children. Being curious will make you and this company great.	Do I understand the first principles of this problem and can I use them to design a better solution?

HEADLINE	DESCRIPTION	QUESTION
Focused on scale, but willing to do things that don't	Sometimes the best way to reach scale in the long term is to do things that don't in the short term.	If I look back on this decision in the future will I regret doing something that didn't scale?
Led by product	Product is not just what we build, it's the way we are. Everyone in the company should be thinking in, and building, products.	Can I find a way to automate or productize the work I'm doing right now?
Not just a job	We want you to look back and feel that Percolate put your career on a new trajectory. You are proud, and you wouldn't change a thing.	Does this decision move me closer towards my personal mission and vision?
Just	At Percolate you are encouraged to run fast, be fearless, and work hard. If you make a mistake, let's all learn from it.	Am I acting in the best interest of the company's values?

WHAT I THINK WORKS ABOUT THESE

Percolate's values are unique, brief, and actionable. You can tell they worked on these and care about what they say.

WHAT I THINK COULD BE IMPROVED

A set of 10 values is two times too many.

We are our choices.

–Jean-Paul Sartre

CHAPTER 4

Behaviors

L ike layers of sediment over time, our decisions stack one on the next to make us who we are. The same is true for business, but more so. An organization is the accumulation of every choice made by every employee. And while any single act may seem to have little effect overall, together they can make or break a company.

This shouldn't be surprising to experienced executives. It is the very definition of a leader to increase the number of good choices made throughout his or her organization. Behaviors that move the business closer to its goals—those that are honest, build trust, and improve team performance—are noble, but that doesn't make them easy. Like in our personal lives, it takes energy to consistently make good choices.

But when we don't have the energy, those beneficial behaviors lose out. Most times weary travelers of life take the path of least resistance, even if that path is heading in the wrong direction. Avoiding confrontation and indecision cost a lot less in effort than honest conversation and decisive action. When exhausted, ego can take charge, and we react from emotion, not logic. Health experts around the world have come to understand the concept of energy conservation and its impact on behavior—sleep is now a core ingredient in any proper nutrition program. When working late, how many times have you ordered the steamed broccoli instead of the pizza?

An organization is the accumulation of every choice made by every employee.

Most employees don't want to undermine the company, of course. When they are at their best, reasonable people will make choices that benefit the organization. The problem is that the pace of work is rarely conducive to us being at our best. Too often there are too many fires, and too little time to get it all done. In the manic, demanding world in which we live, poor behavior doesn't need a lot of fuel to start. And once poor behavior begins, it can create a vicious cycle that is hard to break because, as it turns out, poor behavior might be contagious.

Behaviors
Choices made by employees that are guided by purpose and values.

THE IMITATION GAME

Have you ever noticed a married couple that looks similar? Or when a child acts like his or her parent? Or how a gaggle of teens talk with similar lilts? It's because of "The Chameleon Effect,"[1] a strategy we Homo sapiens have learned over thousands of years to foster acceptance and success. Spend enough time with someone and we unknowingly emulate their postures, mannerisms, and facial expressions.

To gain approval in communities we learn which words to use (for the cocktail party set it's "Mrs.," but for surfers it's "dude"); what to wear (on a Harley you wear leather, but on a bike you wear spandex); and even when to show up. (Don't walk into the opera 45 minutes late like you might for a hip-hop show.)

In fact, the tactic is so ingrained in our reptilian brain that as risks and rewards rise so does our reliance on this phenomenon. Behaviors spread rapidly at work, and this is why.

The workplace, physical or virtual, has nearly all the conditions needed to activate our tendency toward mimicry. It is a high-risk, high-reward environment. There are few dangers greater than failure at work for most people, and not many rewards better than a promotion. Add to this equation the sheer number of hours we spend with coworkers, and the office becomes the perfect environment for breeding behavior chameleons.

Think about it in your own work environment. Do coworkers use business jargon that anyone outside the office would think of as weird to say? Is there an unofficial dress code popular with managers? If these easily observable affects have taken hold, imagine the prevalence of less-obvious decision-making trends.

Behaviors are powerful influencers at work. They are the fuel for strategy, the tools to recruit, and the evidence of ideals made real. Behaviors effect how management communicates with employees, and how products are designed and developed. Wherever there are humans, there are thousands of behaviors that move the company.

But actions that benefit the company spread as easily as those that hurt it, which is why it is a leader's most important job to create the guardrails that tip the balance in favor of the good. If you want to move your organization in a positive and consistent direction, you need to understand that behaviors are the fundamental building block of business.

STRATEGY STARTS WITH BEHAVIORS; BEHAVIORS START WITH STRATEGY

When DigitalOcean tripled in size between 2014 and 2016, its leaders were compelled to think more intentionally about behaviors and how they aligned with the company strategy. Ben Uretsky, the cofounder and CEO of the successful cloud platform provider, knew that this extreme growth only made the technology industry's imperative of constant iteration more pressing. To keep up, the company leaders concluded employees had to learn all about continuous learning: how to go about doing it, and how to be motivated to take responsibility for

egy starts with behaviors star

it. They wanted to become a "growth mindset" organization. (DigitalOcean doesn't call "growth mindset" one of their values, but I would.) It became clear that the behaviors their leaders wanted from their culture were all rooted in this single concept.

DigitalOcean needed a program to inspire the behaviors that would help people inside their organization become experts in the concept of continuous growth. Rich Vincent, director of Talent and Organizational Development at DigitalOcean, points out that at DigitalOcean they believe that "all employees are capable of learning, growing, and innovating, and it's our responsibility to unlock their full potential." They decided that building an internal coaching capability would be the best way to achieve this.

Typically, executive coaching employs tools of reflection to help individuals increase their self-awareness to improve their interpersonal skills and performance at work.

DigitalOcean brought this skill in-house, where managers have become the key players, taking on the role and responsibility of coaching individuals on their teams.

Matt Hoffman, VP of People at DigitalOcean, observed that the managers who are the best coaches often have coaches themselves. He's learned that "when the capacity of managers to be better coaches increases, so too does the capacity of the teams that work for them." Regularly scheduled events keep the program on track, and every individual sets and reviews

ith strategy starts with beha

goals quarterly with his or her manager. This, in combination with a stream of continuous feedback from peers in between these benchmarks, creates a system that elevates the quality and frequency beyond what an external coach or team of coaches could ever hope to do.

The program has had a huge impact on DigitalOcean's culture and business. As coaching took hold, teams worked together more, customer service improved, and employees reported that they were more engaged, and more likely to stay longer. They've even hired Rachel Rider, a full-time talent and performance coach to accelerate the effects of a growth mindset. This is amazing for a company just shy of 500 employees.

DigitalOcean's Talent and Organizational Development organization is responsible for ensuring that people get healthy feedback that is useful and transformative. As part of the team, Rachel partners directly with both high performers and potential underperformers to address individual-, team-, or organization-level challenges.

For DigitalOcean coaching has an added benefit: each person knows that he or she matters to the company. When employees feel seen and respected as contributing members of the company, they respond by living up to that image of themselves, becoming better people and more productive workers.

DigitalOcean is far from perfect. But that's the point. The entire organization is growing and learning through thoughtfully designed behaviors and the impact of its developmental-focused approach is clear in the company's growth and performance. Every employee at every level is constantly making choices that move the business closer to, or further from, its goals.

CULTURE IS THE RESULT OF EVERY CHOICE, BIG AND SMALL.

For example:

- How are meetings run, and how often?

- How do managers mentor new associates?

- Are the contributions of employees recognized?

- Do employees get a voice in how their work environments are designed?

GROWTH MINDSET BEHAVIORS

What might behaviors inspired by a growth mindset look like?

1. *Take a class to learn a new skill, and then share what you learned.* Even though DigitalOcean is stocked with a sea of developers I can imagine there are probably a few employees who aren't code savvy. Why not choose to learn a little Python or Objective-C to better understand the customer and the work they do?

2. *Practice listening.* Too often in conversations people focus on what they will say next rather than hearing what is being said. Improve your communication skills by listening better. Set a reminder on your phone to bug you at least once a day with a note to practice this skill in the next conversation you have.

3. *Bring in outside inspiration.* It's easy to get trapped in the bubble of work. Establish a lunch-and-learn series where experts from outside the company and the field are brought in to share what they know. Not only is it a break from the regular humdrum, it can spark new ideas and inspire continued learning.

4. *Regularly question assumptions about a product you might be working on.* At a company like DigitalOcean, regularly setting aside time every few months to observe market trends and ask what it means for the company can be a great way to avoid a presumption rut. If 56 percent of traffic to the Internet's most visited sites now comes from mobile devices what might that mean for their services? How will it change how customers sign up for a product?

FINDERS KEEPERS

When it comes to finding and keeping great people, it's war. In cities and industries where the market for talent is so tight, even good money doesn't go very far. Every HR exec is trying to better his or her recruiting and retention with new strategies. However, only those who go beyond headhunting and job posting to culture design will succeed. That's the approach Greenhouse Software, an applicant tracking and recruiting software company, took.

Almost from day one, Greenhouse experienced the enviable growth of a successful start-up. In their second year of business, they quadrupled in size from 45 to 175 employees and from 400 to 1,200 clients. *In. One. Year.*

Behind extreme growth like this lurks an extreme challenge: how to get the right people in the doors and keep them on track so the culture survives. Staring this hypergrowth in the face, Greenhouse's VP of Strategy and Marketing, Maia Josebachvili, got to work. To encourage behaviors that delivered on the company values (a credo, in their world) Maia and her team focused on the moments that would have the most influence. They identified four touchpoints along the employee experience lifecycle: *recruitment, onboarding, recognition,* and *assessment.* Even attempts at small behavior change throughout an organization are a big task. Wisely, they tackled each moment one at a time.

SAY BUT DON'T DO

False promises that
lead to failing trust
in leadership and
disregard for initiatives.

SAY AND DO

Culture Gold!

DON'T SAY DON'T DO

Behaviors that are
not part of our culture.

DON'T SAY BUT DO

Implicit behaviors
are problematic because
they need to be shared
and codified to scale.

BEHAVIORS ARE THE CENTER POINT

OF EVERY CULTURE. AS LEADERS, MAKE SURE YOU

DO WHAT YOU SAY AND SAY WHAT YOU DO.

THE GREENHOUSE PLAN

The team's first to-do was to rewrite their *recruiting score-card*, a simple template that lists the elements that the role requires. Next to the elements, the options—a thumbs-up, a thumbs-sideways, or a thumbs-down—are placed. If employees are going to live their values, they realized all potential employees have to be screened for those traits in addition to specific skills and qualifications. They added their values to the recruiting scorecard.

The methodology of sorting for values fit, in addition to technical competency, is gaining popularity in recruiting circles more broadly. Even so, Greenhouse has taken it one step further. Maia explains:

> For all candidates who make it on-site for an interview, we have a specific culture-add interview that is always conducted by someone on a different team who has no direct investment into whether the role gets filled that day. . . . If someone is technically competent but wouldn't add to our culture and align with our values—for example, they're not collaborative—we don't make an offer.

Next, Maia and her team tackled onboarding as a channel to train new and current employees on values and their related behaviors. They designed a comprehensive *culture education module* that includes opportunities to define what the values mean in terms of each person's day-to-day decisions.

Two reasons I love this:

1. While most organizations see the goal of onboarding as sharing logistics and general orientation, new employees are most attentive and excited during their first 30 days. It is *the perfect* occasion to introduce and indoctrinate newbies, which is clearly the opportunity Greenhouse hits hard.

2. Values aren't enacted by the company as a whole, but by individuals one at a time. It's critical that every individual understands that he or she is responsible for living the values in his or her own way. Clearly the company does have a role to play and Greenhouse steps up to explain this concept and their expectations.

Next, Maia's team brought values-based behaviors to life by designing everyday moments that reinforced these ideas. For example, they began celebrating accomplishments at the all-hands meetings in the context of their credo. This is a perfect example of the type of recognition we'll get into more in the next chapter.

And finally, to measure the effectiveness of these redesigned employee experiences, the People team began asking questions about each element in the companywide engagement survey. This was critical to keep themselves in check, evaluate if their work was having an impact, and determine if the values were staying relevant as the company evolved.

GREENHOUSE BEHAVIOR TOUCHPOINTS

1. Evaluate candidates on values alignment.

2. Onboard with value-behavior education.

3. Celebrate values-based accomplishments.

4. Assess program, behaviors, and values.

Through the process of redesigning key moments in the employee life cycle the team learned that at Greenhouse culture wasn't about words, it was about behaviors. If you asked an employee to describe what it's like to work at Greenhouse, almost everyone would share a moment that exemplifies the company values. Over time, the retelling of these moments have become the core of their company's culture.

UNITED BEHAVIORS OF PURPOSE

Behaviors are complicated gremlins. But even in the most complex organizations they can be wrangled when connected to culture. Greenhouse uses their values to inform behaviors, but purpose can be a powerful driver as well. In fact, any purpose statement worth the laptop it's written on should, in some way, inform how companies make choices. This culture rule of thumb is as true for nonprofits as it is for for-profit companies; as applicable to young start-ups as it is to evergreen blue-chip companies; and as important for enterprises as it is for community institutions. Purpose can help people make culturally-aligned choices even at universities where students, educators, and staff come together with few shared incentives.

Long an outlier among business schools, the Yale School of Management, or SOM, was founded in 1976. The program's original degree, a Master's in Public and Private Administration, was ditched many years ago, but its original purpose still stands: "*To educate leaders for business and society.*" These seven words tell students and the world the philosophy on which it was founded: the public and private sectors are inextricably linked. This purpose might be obvious now as more businesses see the benefit of social impact, but it was an astounding belief for a business program of the mid-1970s.

One of the most profound behaviors the SOM purpose inspires is the nearly universal support of *The Internship Fund*. This program provides financial assistance to any student who takes a public sector or nonprofit summer internship with little or no pay and needs help to make ends meet. The student spending his or her summer at an education advocacy organization earns a lot less than his or her classmate at a management consultancy, but everyone in the program believes both paths are equally valuable. Which is why it's the students themselves who donate the cash that makes the fund possible. Every year since the fund's inception, nearly 100 percent of the SOM student body

> To find specific examples of ideal behaviors, talk to the peers of your Culture All-Stars . Ask which choices make each All-Star a great colleague, and which positive behaviors have spread throughout their team.

donates to ensure that no classmate would have to skip a summer opportunity because of financial repercussions.

The belief in the value of public and private enterprises is benchmarked in the school's purpose and lived across the organization through students who commit hundreds—and in some cases thousands—of dollars. They do so not because they will be recognized, not because they are supporting their friends, but because donating is one of the ways that SOM celebrates their unique culture. It is a behavior that helps them collectively realize their community's purpose of educating leaders for business and society.

ACTIVATION STATION

Behaviors are the core of culture and the key to business. At Greenhouse, Maia and her team learned that when redesigning their employee experience, the founders at DigitalOcean proved it to be true with their coaching practice. The students at the Yale School of Management display it every semester through *The Internship Fund*. Whether to help the organization improve how they learn, how to get and keep the right people, or make culturally-aligned choices when incentives are diverse, by tapping into the steadying force of purpose and values, leaders can identify the behaviors that will chart a course for business through the tumult of twenty-first-century business.

Culture isn't shaped by one choice, but 10,000 decisions.

But knowing where you want to go and getting there are two very different tasks. Purpose, values, and behaviors define what we hope our culture will be, but how do we make sure that everyone has a clear picture of what an ideal culture-driven behavior is? Point to the ones that are already happening, which is exactly the role that recognition should play in your culture.

Behaviors Quick-Start

Identify which behaviors are good for your culture and which ones aren't.

HOW SHOULD EMPLOYEES ACT?

Decide What You Will Stop, Start, and Continue

Assemble about 15 formal and informal leaders from across the organization, ideally your Culture All-Stars. This team will help evaluate, identify, and prioritize three types of team and organizational behaviors: (1) those that aren't representative of the company's values and purpose, (2) those that do align with the company's values and purpose, and (3) those that, if introduced, would be ideal examples of the company's values and purpose.

With your group, use the following tools to list and rank the three categories of behaviors. For this exercise it's important to use a canvas on which everyone can work together. I like giant sticky pads over whiteboards because the work can stay visible around the room. It's not ideal, but this exercise can be done remotely. If you do choose to go remote, use an online collaboration tool like Google Sheets or Trello.

Now, establish three work areas, one for each category, and fill each according to the instructions on the following pages. Once complete, discuss what you will need to end "Stop" items, ways to celebrate "Continue" items, and how to implement critical "Start" items.

WHY YOU'RE DOING THIS
To evaluate, identify, and prioritize three types of behaviors.

HOW YOU'LL DO IT
A half-day workshop.

WHO SHOULD PARTICIPATE
8 to 15 Culture All-Stars.

WHERE IT SHOULD HAPPEN
A large room with lots of wall space and room to collaborate.

WHAT YOU'LL NEED
White boards or poster-sized sticky pads, a few regular-sized Post-it pads, markers, pens, and a set of worksheets for each participant. If you are facilitating this exercise remotely, use an online collaboration tool like Google Sheets or Trello.

HOW LONG YOU'LL NEED
3 hours.

Download this exercise to work on with your team at **greatmondays.com**

GREENHOUSE CULTURE CREDO

AUTHENTIC
- We act and talk like real people.
- We are honest, candid, and sincere with our customers and colleagues.

EFFECTIVE
- We are purposeful in the focus of our efforts.
- We have a strong bias for action.
- We deliver.

CUSTOMER-FOCUSED
- We care about the success of our customers.
- We are thoughtful about delivering a positive customer experience.
- We act in the long-term best interests of our customers.

INCLUSIVE AND OPEN-MINDED
- We are committed to an environment where people from a diversity of backgrounds feel included and comfortable.
- We encourage different perspectives and opinions.

COLLABORATIVE
- We work toward common goals.
- We trust and help each other.

AMBITIOUS
- We challenge ourselves and each other to do great work.
- We empower people to do the best work of their career.

PART 1: STOP

Part 1 is intended to uncover individual or group behaviors that aren't representative of the company culture you want.

If the majority of participants are together in person:

1. Ask your team to write down as many non-values aligned behaviors as they can on small sticky notes, one idea per note. *Time:* 15 minutes

2. Then have team members present their list to the group, sticking their suggestions on the board as they do. If someone else in the group has the same or a closely-related behavior, have that team member add the behavior to the board next to the first post. *Time:* 30 minutes

If the majority of participants are remote:

1. Instruct each person to take 15 minutes to list individual, team, or corporate behaviors that conflict with the company values in the online tool like Google Sheets or Trello.

2. Collect and organize the responses, grouping any similar or related responses together.

Both in person and remote participants continue here:

3. Once everyone has made their contribution, reflect on the results by asking questions about *patterns*. Which behaviors were most often repeated? Which were single occurrences? Why might this be? By observing patterns, you can learn more about the current state of the organization's culture. For example: Are there a lot of comments about micromanagement? Why might that be? Does that support or challenge assumptions about your culture?
   Time: 30 minutes

Ranking

4. On a scale of 1 to 3, assign two numbers to each behavior.

   The first number will indicate how urgent the undesirable behavior is. If in person, split up the behaviors and ask participants to help score a few each.
   - 1 is a behavior that is least urgent ("This isn't ideal, but it isn't critical.")
   - 3 is a behavior that is most urgent ("We've got to stop this immediately.")

   The second number will represent how much effort will be required to stop that behavior.

   - 1 is a behavior that will be harder to stop
   - 3 is a behavior that will be easier to stop

   Time: 10 minutes

5. Tally your numbers, then prioritize the items with the highest totals.

LIST INDIVIDUAL AND GROUP BEHAVIORS THAT AREN'T REPRESENTATIVE OF THE COMPANY'S VALUES.

Behaviors to stop:	HOW URGENT? 1 2 3	HOW EASY? 1 2 3	TOTAL
_____	○○○	○○○	_____
_____	○○○	○○○	_____
_____	○○○	○○○	_____
_____	○○○	○○○	_____
_____	○○○	○○○	_____
_____	○○○	○○○	_____
_____	○○○	○○○	_____
_____	○○○	○○○	_____

PART 2: CONTINUE

Part 2 is intended to identify existing behaviors that should continue. This section will help employees have a clear picture of what positive behavior looks like in your company.

6. Follow the same process as in Part 1 for behaviors within the organization that support the culture you want to create.
    Time: 60 minutes

Ranking

7. List and rank the behaviors in order of their clarity of connection to your organization's purpose or values, and the amount of energy or resources they take.

    On a scale of 1 to 3, assign two numbers to each behavior. The first number will indicate how aligned the behavior is to your organization's purpose or values.

    - 1 is a behavior that is least aligned ("This is a positive behavior, but it doesn't map to any of our values or purpose.")
    - 3 is a behavior that is most aligned ("This behavior directly contributes to living our values and achieving our purpose.")

    Time: 10 minutes

The second number represents how much effort it will require to support the behavior.

- 1 is a behavior that takes a lot of time, energy, or budget to keep going
- 3 is a behavior that happens easily, without needing much organizational support

Time: 10 minutes

8. Tally your numbers. While all the items on this list are good in some way, the behaviors with the highest number will be the most important to focus on.

LIST INDIVIDUAL AND GROUP BEHAVIORS THAT SUPPORT THE COMPANY'S VALUES.

Behaviors to continue:	HOW ALIGNED? ① ② ③	HOW EASY? ① ② ③	TOTAL
_____	◯ ◯ ◯	◯ ◯ ◯	_____
_____	◯ ◯ ◯	◯ ◯ ◯	_____
_____	◯ ◯ ◯	◯ ◯ ◯	_____
_____	◯ ◯ ◯	◯ ◯ ◯	_____
_____	◯ ◯ ◯	◯ ◯ ◯	_____
_____	◯ ◯ ◯	◯ ◯ ◯	_____
_____	◯ ◯ ◯	◯ ◯ ◯	_____
_____	◯ ◯ ◯	◯ ◯ ◯	_____

PART 3: START

Part 3 is a bit harder. It's the same process as above, but this time the task is to imagine new behaviors that aren't happening now but should be. These are activities that if introduced into the organization would help employees better act on its purpose or values. Imagining what doesn't exist is a difficult task, so make sure you've recruited a few people for whom this is a talent. Designers and creatives of any kind are ideal candidates.

9. Ask each person to generate as many new value-driven behaviors as possible. Instruct them to start with the first value and imagine choices that individuals, managers, groups, and the organization could make that would support that value. *Hint: ask participants about ideal behaviors they've seen at other companies. What could your company do that is similar?*
   Time: 10 minutes

10. Have each participant share their ideas with the group, allow time for others to add ideas as they come up. Make sure to record these new ideas as well.
    Time: 10 minutes

11. Move to the next value and repeat the process of working individually then sharing with the group.
    Time: 20 minutes per value

12. Continue until all the values have been addressed.

13. Assign each participant someone else's ideas to rank.

Ranking

14. Like Part 2, on a scale of 1 to 3, assign two numbers to each behavior. The first number will indicate how aligned the new behavior is to purpose and values.

- 1 is a behavior that is least aligned
- 3 is a behavior that is most aligned

Time: 10 minutes

15. The second number represents how much effort might be required to introduce and support the behavior. I say *might* because you won't really know until you've done it, so make an informed guess.

- 1 is a new behavior that will take a lot of time, energy, and/or budget to initiate and support
- 3 is a new behavior that will probably not need a big push to get it started, nor much organizational support to run

Time: 10 minutes

16. Tally your numbers. The behaviors with the top three scores are your high-leverage points. Without too much effort, these should move your organization toward the culture you want. Time to start implementing.

LIST ANY BEHAVIORS THAT AREN'T OCCURRING BUT SHOULD BECAUSE THEY WOULD HELP THE COMPANY ACT ON ITS VALUES.

Behaviors to start:	HOW ALIGNED? ① ② ③	HOW EASY? ① ② ③	TOTAL
_____	○○○	○○○	_____
_____	○○○	○○○	_____
_____	○○○	○○○	_____
_____	○○○	○○○	_____
_____	○○○	○○○	_____
_____	○○○	○○○	_____
_____	○○○	○○○	_____
_____	○○○	○○○	_____

Brains, like hearts,
go where they are
appreciated.

—Robert McNamara

Recognition

Dogs. Chimps. Humans. We're a lot alike. In addition to our four-chambered heart and love of social interaction, advanced mammals share the need for positive reinforcement. Managers have used this trait to motivate employees since the first sales organization crawled out of the water to attend its inaugural awards dinner.

But if sales are the only metric, under the right *wrong* circumstances loyal lieutenants will do anything to achieve their goal, including cheating. In 2016, Wells Fargo managers opened tens of thousands of fake or unauthorized accounts when pressured to increase the bank's stock price through sales activity. In 2014, it was discovered that Volkswagen created algorithms to cheat emissions testing so they could sell more diesel cars in North America.

For decades, "Sell more and you'll be rich" was the charge. Today's version might be "ship faster" or "capture clicks," but the message to the employee is the same: the organization has only one immediate need and it's your job to get us there. Solely rewarding behaviors that drive short-term corporate

Recognition
Programs that applaud and encourage behaviors that support the culture.

wins over long-term customer benefits can cause serious damage to a company's reputation. How can leaders avoid these PR nightmares? Simple: Reward behaviors connected to company values.

HOIST THE CARROT

The problem with most recognition programs is that they reward the wrong things. Of course, sales is important, but every business outcome is the result of how people work. The best way to achieve those goals consistently (and honestly) is recognizing behaviors that lead to those results, not the results themselves. Attempting to shortcut the cycle by rewarding only the outcome leads to dangerous choices and dysfunctional cultures. Incentivizing employees to directly influence the result is like paying babysitters for how much food they get your kids to eat. It might be effective at first, but eventually how they do the rest of their job suffers.

Incentivizing employees to directly influence results is like paying a babysitter for how much food they get your kid to eat.

For culture design to take hold, leaders must recognize and reward values-driven choices. Pointing out an individual or team will make employees proud of what they did and continue that behavior. And because of their mammalian tendencies, others in the organization will see this positive recognition and emulate that behavior, too.

Rewarding values hoists the carrot further up the cause-and-effect chain and away from outcomes. But be careful not to go too far. For all its inspirational power, purpose isn't useful here. Individuals and teams can't be rewarded for something only the organization as a whole can achieve. That, and reaching your purpose doesn't happen frequently enough to be useful. Remember the story of Adaptive Path from Chapter 2? It took them 10 years to achieve theirs—and that was quick. The best we can do is reward the behaviors that will help get us there.

Tap your Culture All-Stars for help when starting any type of recognition program. They'll understand what you are trying to do. They can nominate, present awards, and be individuals who step up and provide recognition off-the-cuff. Recognition also presents a great opportunity to start growing the ranks of your All-Stars. Who regularly tops the list of reward receivers *and* givers? Bring them in informally by asking them to advise on other culture initiatives or formally by welcoming them in with a small token. (Congrats! Here's your new Culture All-Star pin).

THE FOUR TYPES OF RECOGNITION

Believe it or not, there are more effective ways to recognize people than the usual cash, trips, and trophies. And while some companies think they're stepping up their rewards with new improvements to old methods like team-based "pro-social" awards, they're missing a bigger opportunity. Four opportunities, actually. For a team, business unit, or organization to live a company's values beyond awards nomination month, leaders need to identify and fulfill all four types.

To understand the different kinds of recognition, I split them along two axes. The first axis is defined by *the person doing the recognizing*. Is he or she a leader or a peer? The second axis is defined by *the person who created the program*. Did the program spring from the head of an HR manager, or was it from an employee? Map the two axes and you get four kinds of recognition: (1) formal recognition from leadership; (2) formal recognition from peers; (3) informal recognition from peers; and (4) informal recognition from leadership. Let's start with number one.

FORMAL

LEADERSHIP

PEER

INFORMAL

FOR CULTURE DESIGN TO TAKE HOLD,

LEADERS MUST IDENTIFY AND CELEBRATE VALUES-DRIVEN

CHOICES WITH ALL FOUR TYPES OF RECOGNITION.

1. Formal Recognition from Leadership

Congratulations. You've done it, and now you are being recognized by a manager or executive through a program that was created by the company. These are the most common kinds of initiatives and they can include old standbys, like awards dinners. But they can also get more interesting.

In the early 2000s, I was part of a team that ran a global recognition program for Hewlett-Packard called The CIRCLE Awards. Its goal was to incentivize design and innovation in all forms. We would help HP put out a call for entries, film the judges, host a celebratory dinner, and bestow the trophies. Marketing, products, partnerships—if it was a new approach that could prove some benefit to the company, it was celebrated. Participation in the program grew as year after year, winners became case studies, which would inspire others to enter, ultimately spreading the word that the company fully supported new ideas and experiments.

HP awarded cash bonuses and stock for the first few years, but even when those perks were curbed the excitement and impact remained intact. The awards were an exciting opportunity to elevate and share the best stories, and it happened every year for almost a decade.

Formal leadership recognition doesn't have to be on a grand scale like HP, though. David Kahn, former VP of Human Resources at Rendina, a small healthcare real estate developer in the Southeast, shared one of the most important parts of the recognition program he ran. Leading up to the Core Value Awards, or CVAs, every employee at Rendina votes for a coworker who has embodied one of the corporate values from the past year. Once selected, winners are announced publicly by the CEO at the State of The Company Address.

David points out that during the event "we share all the ways each winner has personified the core value" which is equally as important as the CEO pronouncement from on high. This piece of Rendina's CVAs creates a domino effect of engagement. Employees are part of the selection process, which nudges each person to think about and internalize the meaning of the core values, and that results in the sharing of the behaviors that support the values. Being an organization under 200 employees, Rendina's CVAs don't have the pomp of MTV's Video Music Awards, but they don't need to. The process of getting to the awards is designed to work as hard to increase awareness and engagement across the company as the awards themselves.

Formal leader-driven recognition programs are great because they give the company heads a lot of control over what is rewarded and how, but they also have their challenges. Designing a companywide program that doesn't come off as fake is tough. The goal when designing any large-scale initiative created for employees is that the majority of the community embraces it.

When creating a Quadrant 1 recognition program, don't just assume an awards dinner is the best solution. Think about the people in the organization. For a more buttoned-up organization, presenting a trophy in front of peers may work. But if your teams are more casual, maybe a round of drinks at a karaoke bar would do the trick. How might you recognize the behaviors you want in a way that fits your culture?

FORMAL FROM LEADERSHIP

Is it supported?   Share a clear plan with outcomes to
your executive team and get their buy-in
before starting.

Is it authentic?   Your program should feel like it was designed
for your company, not just slapped together.
If the program doesn't feel authentic,
employees are less likely to participate.

Is it explained?   Everyone who could be recognized needs
to know they are part of it, even if they don't
win. Share what they can expect, how they
can take part, and why it's happening.

Is it consistent?   One and done won't do. To be effective,
behaviors should be rewarded consistently,
even if the format changes.

2. Formal Recognition from Peers

Peer-to-peer (P2P) recognition gives leaders a tool to encourage value-driven behaviors without fancy awards and dollar pay-outs. Not that bonuses are being refused, but people respond just as well to praise accompanied by symbols that hold no monetary benefit to the individual. Formal P2P recognition is a regular opportunity for colleagues to acknowledge one another. It's not only cost-effective, fostering regular compliments on work across the team strengthens relationships and builds trust. The appreciator also gets something. People who practice appreciation tend to be more empathetic and less aggressive. Not a bad set of attributes for any workplace to have.

DonorsChoose.org, a nonprofit that allows individuals to donate directly to public school classroom projects, has always made gratitude a major part of their culture. From the small DonorsChoose.org gift cards they send to teacher-volunteers to the handwritten thank-you notes they send to every staff member during the holidays, recognition is built into the culture. But a few years back they created a program that lets peers recognize one another.

It started when YouEarnedIt, an employee recognition-and-reward software company, asked DonorsChoose.org to create a customized experience for one of their customers. Together, they designed a process through which employees could earn recognition points and then cash them in for DonorsChoose.org gift cards. "We loved this idea so much we decided to use it internally," explained Melanie Duppins, DonorsChoose.org's former VP of People Operations. By translating their recognition from analog to digital they could scale the practice and make it easier for team members to thank one another more frequently.

DonorsChoose.org's employees can now go to the YouEarnedIt platform and recognize a peer who has gone above and beyond, then tag that shout-out with one of their core values. Other people who see it can add their support through high fives (their version of a thumbs-up) and pile on additional points and comments.

Melanie told me about a time she was thanked through the program:

> I received recognition when I shared our employee survey results at an all-hands meeting. Even though it was difficult, I was forthcoming about the areas where we needed to improve as an organization. A junior person on our team recognized me, saying that she appreciated my humility when sharing survey results. She tagged it with our core value of transparency.

This is a terrific example of a well-functioning formal P2P recognition system.

There are plenty of digital tools that facilitate P2P callouts like YouEarnedIt. And while more platforms are starting to enable philanthropic rewards like DonorsChoose.org, too often points can be redeemed for prizes, which sends the wrong message. (Do this, get that.) But even with extrinsic motivators these tools are still valuable; they track and tally patterns of employee choice revealing what might otherwise be hard to see. Help employees remember the intent of the program by pointing out behaviors that were rewarded on the platform in real life, too.

Software is tricky though, so if you go this route, here are some warnings:

1. People will be tempted to find work-arounds. In my experience, engineers, in particular, find gaming the system too tempting to ignore.
2. Watch out for point inflation.
3. When recognition becomes easy people may need guidance.

Melanie points out that in her experience employees tend to blow through their points too quickly. Do you authorize more to support ALL this positive behavior or encourage budgeting? Be cautious with your points. In our always-on lives, we become desensitized to regular digital stimulus (like your overflowing inbox, for example) in order to cope. Each additional point piled on has less value until eventually they mean nothing. What begins with good intention can end in point bloat and another digital tool that is willfully ignored. ::uninstalls app::

With the right intent and a well-executed rollout, apps can be a great addition to any suite of recognition tools. But when choosing a digital tool, make sure it plays the role of supporting strategy, not *being* the strategy.

RECOGNITION CHECKLIST:
FORMAL FROM PEERS

Is it believable?   If people are going to make the effort, they
need to believe in its benefits.

Is it understood?   Be clear about what behaviors derived from
values look like. Point out existing examples.

Is it consistent?   Make sure managers and team leads are
committed to helping people regularly
recognize one another.

3. Informal Recognition from Peers

I don't know about you, but I never get tired of compliments.
It's a well of rewards that never runs dry. If someone at work
is inspired to tell you how amazing your contribution to that
last product launch was, well, that's one of the best feelings in
the world. Informal recognition from peers requires little fore-
thought, and costs nothing. Of course, a pat on the back will
work fine, but there's no reason we can't get creative. An anon-
ymous note, a handmade certificate for coffee and scones, and
a superlative-inscribed flag cut from card stock flying above
a colleague's cube are all cheap, all a thrill, and all incredibly
effective. For those who are digitally inclined or have peers in
more than one location, every one of these can be translated
nicely over email, Slack, or even, gasp! by real mail.

A great informal recognition system emerged in the early days at Delivering Happiness. The team at this Zappos spin-off wanted a way to celebrate their culture and each other. They decided gifting a bacon-shaped pillow to the person who best lived a company value was the way to go. The bacon was passed from winner to winner, presented in front of the team so they could all celebrate the new owner. Originally the winner was chosen by the previous pillow-holder, but as the program evolved it became more democratic. They started an email address for nominations. If a member of the team saw his or her peer do something great they could shoot a note saying so to bacon@deliveringhappiness and it would be recorded.

I love the bacon pillow example for a lot of reasons, but mostly because the reward, if you can call it that, is so silly. Tchotchkes, meaningless tokens, have little tangible value but hold a lot in the way of social capital.

Earnest motivation is what makes informal P2P effective, but once the habit begins to have a positive effect, it might evolve. That's great. Let it. The bacon pillow started as a simple low-key celebration but changed when voting became more systemized. In some ways it's almost the point to prototype informal recognition and if it works, let it become a more formal initiative.

One challenge to look out for: too much meddling or formalizing from corporate and the earnest quality may become hollow. How should a company encourage informal recognition without ruining it? The best thing outside observers can do is nod in approval and ask how they can help.

WHAT DOES GOOD INFORMAL P2P RECOGNITION LOOK LIKE?

Be specific.

Connect it to an action they took, and the value it expressed.

Be near.

Pay the compliment shortly after the behavior happened.

Be heartfelt.

Dig deep and mean what you say.

When changing habits of a team to encourage compliments, leaders can build momentum by sharing the importance of P2P recognition, the intention behind it, and then lead by example. When starting out, creating your own recognition triggers can help. It could be an arbitrary reminder like always telling someone different how much he or she is appreciated as you head out to grab that afternoon coffee. Or you can connect the trigger to accomplishments like starting and completing phases of work, creatively celebrating how a person contributed.

Informal P2P recognition is hard to start, but easy to keep up. The behavior is cheap. If Delivering Happiness can pass around a bacon pillow to reinforce behaviors, then anyone can design a good P2P recognition program.

RECOGNITION CHECKLIST:
INFORMAL FROM PEERS

Is it effective?   Teach your team how to be praise pros and give compliments well.

Is it understood?   Be clear about what behaviors derived from values look like. Point out existing examples.

Is it creative?   Like a good birthday gift, a little thought goes a long way.

Is it consistent?   It's going to take practice to make this part of your team's regular routine. Keep at it and you'll be living your values in no time.

4. Informal Recognition from Leadership

Can I buy you lunch? There isn't a better string of words in English. And coming from a manager makes it that much better. Any team leader can spend a little time and money acknowledging great work choices, all the while deepening trust and rapport. Even a quick coffee with a manager goes a long way.

These high-touch moments of recognition from leadership carry a lot of weight. They provide the time to be more explicit about a particular outcome or pattern of decisions. Once the latte is poured, chatting about an individual's values-inspired choice and how it supported the team and company can fuel an employee for weeks. But the short-term morale boost isn't the only reason to spend time listing an employee's great choices. It's a compelling way for leaders to reaffirm that values are important, not just in theory, but in a real way for the team. Informal recognition from a leader says to the employee that he is seen, appreciated, and that his choices matter.

It can be tough to find the time to continually take a team to coffee one at a time, so if you need to dial down the time commitment, even shooting out a quick but meaningful email can do. A friend at AppDynamics happily shares stories about the manager who sends thank-you emails to her team acknowledging their contributions. How easy is that?

Often, informal recognition from leadership like emails or a pat on the back happen away from others. These moments are private, and sometimes that's appropriate. But realize when others don't see it happening, the social power of recognition is muted. Managers should do their best to share callouts within meetings or in front of the group.

Here are some other ways to make informal recognition from leadership visible:

- If a manager takes Shri to a recognition lunch, create a small sign (physical or digital) denoting "I took Shri to lunch for putting in extra hours on Steve's project" and the associated value like "#aboveandbeyond." It makes the event more visible and shareable.
- Setting Slack status is another great spot for an informal recognition note. If you prefer email, include other team members on the thread.
- Other channels for quick social recognition include group texts (I like these because they feel sincere), tweets (excellent for greater exposure), or group stories on Snapchat or Instagram (bonus points for creativity).

RECOGNITION CHECKLIST:
INFORMAL FROM LEADERSHIP

Is it understood? This type of recognition can be time-intensive. Managers need to understand the power and point of one-to-one recognition to sustain the effort over the long term.

Is it creative? New ways of appreciation keep employees interested and thank-yous fresh.

Is it funded? Some cash can go a long way when it comes to coffee and lunches.

MAMMALS WITH HEART

To activate its values, an organization should aim to create all four types of recognition. It's more than likely your organization already has at least one of the four types in place; maybe more that aren't as visible. It's your job to figure out where the organization can do better, discover what kind of thank-yous need to start, and keep an eye out for the recognition that employees are doing all on their own.

When tied to values, recognition will help employees make better decisions, which will in turn lead to happier customers and improve the bottom line. Putting these programs into motion isn't easy. But with effort and time, recognition will grow to become a powerful tool you can use to design a culture that creates results that the business will like and, like any mammal with a heart, employees will love.

Recognition Quick-Start

Inspire values-driven behaviors by designing an ecosystem of recognition programs.

HOW DOES YOUR COMPANY RECOGNIZE GOOD CHOICES?

Catalog Your Existing Recognition Programs

Before you start rewarding values-driven behavior, take an inventory of recognition already in place, determine how to change what they reward, and identify which new types of programs need to be created. In this exercise, you will identify existing programs, determine how you might change each to recognize values-driven behaviors if they aren't already, and design new initiatives for any quadrant that lack activities.

To start, recruit three to five culture co-conspirators from across the organization who have been around the company more than 30 percent of the life of the company. As always, this exercise can be completed remotely, but it's better to do the work at the same time in the same place.

WHY YOU'RE DOING THIS
To create four types of recognition to reward values-driven behaviors.

HOW YOU'LL DO IT
A small-group working session.

WHO SHOULD PARTICIPATE
3 to 5 veteran colleagues.

WHERE IT SHOULD HAPPEN
A medium-sized room with lots of wall space and room to collaborate.

WHAT YOU'LL NEED
A few examples of recognition programs, pens and markers, a collaborative space like a whiteboard, a few standard-sized Post-it pads, and a set of worksheets for each participant including a blank culture recognition matrix.

HOW LONG YOU'LL NEED
2 hours.

Download this exercise to work on with your team at **greatmondays.com**

EXERCISE 1

1. Together, list all the recognition and rewards programs that already occur across your company. Write them down one per sticky note as you go and then post them to the board or wall.
   Time: 20 minutes

2. List your values on the side so you can easily refer to them.
   Time: 5 minutes

3. Of the programs listed, mark the ones that already reward values-based behaviors or those that could if they were changed.
   Time: 15 minutes

4. Draw the recognition 2x2 on the board or wall and place any programs that were marked in the most appropriate of the four quadrants.
   Time: 15 minutes

5. Ask the appropriate questions from one of the four Recognition Checklists for each program. Make a note of the number of "no" answers and any actions you might need to change to turn a "no" to a "yes."
   Time: 30 minutes

WRITE DOWN ALL THE RECOGNITION THAT OCCURS IN YOUR COMPANY.

EXISTING PROGRAMS	YOUR VALUES
List existing rewards and recognition programs.	Write your company values or value themes. 1. 2. 3. 4. 5.

SORT EXISTING RECOGNITION PROGRAMS INTO THEIR APPROPRIATE CATEGORIES.

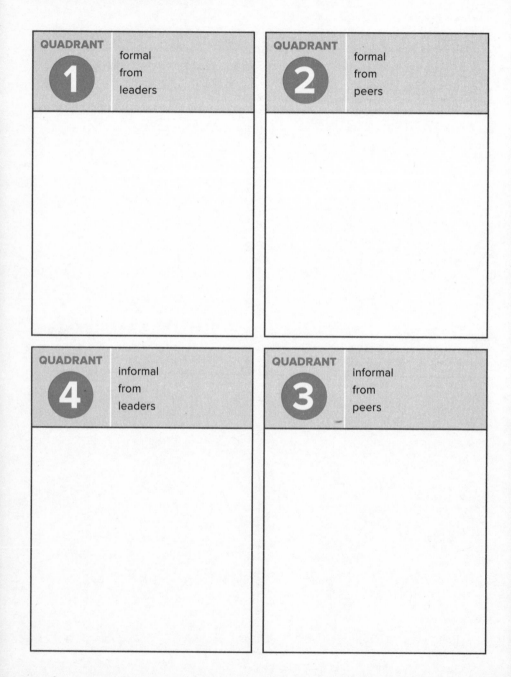

HOW DO YOUR RECOGNITION PROGRAMS ANSWER THEIR KEY QUESTIONS?

QUADRANT **1**	formal from leaders
Recognition program:	
Is it supported?	
Is it authentic?	
Is it explained?	
Is it consistent?	

QUADRANT **2**	formal from peers
Recognition program:	
Is it believable?	
Is it understood?	
Is it consistent?	

QUADRANT **4**	informal from leaders
Recognition program:	
Is it effective?	
Is it understood?	
Is it creative?	
Is it consistent?	

QUADRANT **3**	informal from peers
Recognition program:	
Is it understood?	
Is it funded?	
Is it creative?	

FILL IN THE RECOGNITION GAPS

What behaviors should be rewarded that aren't? In the following exercise, list any value-aligned behavior that isn't being rewarded but should be. Decide with your team which category of recognition might be most appropriate for that value. Can you come up with one example of an existing program in which it could be rewarded? If not, what other ways might this behavior get supported? *Hint: It doesn't have to be a companywide program. Start small within your team or sphere of influence.*

EXERCISE 2

1. On the worksheet to the right, list your company values.
    Time: 5 minutes

2. Fill in one example of an existing behavior not being recognized that aligns with each value.
    Time: 15 minutes

3. Mark which type of recognition might be most appropriate for each value-aligned behavior.
    Time: 10 minutes

4. Work with your colleagues to imagine a new type of recognition program that would reward that behavior. Are there any existing programs in which recognition of this behavior could be included?
    Time: 6 minutes

WHAT'S NEXT?

If any quadrants were empty in the previous exercise, or were weaker than the others, focus on generating ideas for that type to help balance the organization's portfolio of recognition programs.

LIST AN EXISTING BEHAVIOR FOR EACH VALUE AND MARK WHICH CATEGORY OF RECOGNITION IS MOST APPROPRIATE FOR THAT VALUE.

	FORMAL FROM LEADER	FORMAL FROM PEERS	INFORMAL FROM PEERS	INFORMAL FROM LEADERS
value				
behavior				
program	○	○	○	○
value				
behavior				
program	○	○	○	○
value				
behavior				
program	○	○	○	○
value				
behavior				
program	○	○	○	○
value				
behavior				
program	○	○	○	○

Saying hello doesn't
have an ROI. It's
about building
relationships.

—Gary Vaynerchuk

CHAPTER 6

Rituals

If you've ever had to work with another human, you know good relationships make for good work. And while these bonds don't guarantee success, you can be sure it ain't happening without them. Think of relationships as connective tissue; without them businesses would just be a pile of old laptops and ergo chairs. Rituals are the activities that build and strengthen relationships. The more organizations grow, the more they need rituals.

In a modestly-sized organization, a small group of individuals rely on one another to get work done, and usually become a tight-knit bunch in the process. They are an "intimate community"—a group of people where "most of the members recognize and are recognized by many of the others."[1] When individuals develop relationships by nature and necessity, they enable the knowing of the "who's and what's" of the organization. Everyone knows Shelby is the platform expert; Sanjay said we broke our sales records last quarter.

A shared history between people fosters trust. We understand other people's motivations and can probably predict how they'll react. It's a survival technique adapted over thousands of years. But what happens when more and more people show up for work?

Think of relationships as connective tissue; without them businesses would just be a pile of old laptops and ergo chairs.

Whether it's a start-up that has accelerated hiring or a multinational merger, as coworkers increase in number our brains must work harder to remember all the names, faces, and details. Even with the help of new hire emails and fancy interactive organization charts, it's too much to manage. We are forced to choose who we know and how well.

It'll be hardly noticeable at first, but one day soon employees will look up and no longer know all the people that work at the organization. As the percentage of who and what each individual knows diminishes, the relationship of the individual to the company begins to erode.

This is the moment when culture is at its greatest risk of unraveling. If we can see it coming maybe we can prepare for or even prevent it.

Rituals
Activities that build and strengthen relationships.

DR. DUNBAR, I PRESUME?

No experienced CEO will argue that the human side of business isn't critical to success. As groups grow they require more relationship-strengthening activities, or what is known as *social grooming,* to operate effectively. While primates literally groom one another to connect, humans use language as a more efficient method to bond. Over 60 percent of the conversations we have as humans are spent talking about interactions with others and personal experiences.[2] The primary social benefit of this jibber jabber is to learn how others behave, which in turn helps us navigate and build relationships.

Perhaps less time-consuming than picking nits, talking still takes energy. It turns out this energy consumption is what limits our social circles. In 1993, British anthropologist Robin Dunbar concluded[3] that groups can only grow so large. Eventually, the effort it takes to maintain more relationships outweighs the benefit of being together. When the number of individuals grows beyond 150—now known in social psychology as "Dunbar's Number"—the group will divide into subgroups. While the theory is great, there's a problem: when it comes to work, the wheels on the culture wagon get wobbly way before Dunbar might expect.

WHEN CULTURE GOES COCKEYE

Organizing into tribes is the reason apes and their ilk are successful at defending, hunting, and surviving. But at work, the reasons we come together aren't life or death.

Christopher Allen, Internet cryptography pioneer, has tussled with Dunbar's Number in a few well-written articles.[4] He argues that groups subdivide at significantly less than 150; probably around 50, he estimates. Neighborhoods within towns, clans within online communities, and even sports leagues are all groups that self-organize into groups closer to Allen's Number than to Dunbar's. While working at a corporation can evoke fight-or-flight responses, we aren't fending off large toothy predators like our hairier ancestors, even if it sometimes feels like it. Keeping up with people takes energy, and after a while most folks just don't feel like there is any benefit to getting to know someone new. I've got my lunch crew, what else do I need?

Christopher Allen doesn't provide an exact number for this phenomenon, but it doesn't matter. When it comes to relationships weakening (or not happening in the first place), the story is the same nearly every time. If strong relationships aren't fostered, culture is headed off the rails somewhere between 50 and 150 people.

The sooner founders and leaders realize that culture can and should be designed, the sooner they can begin thinking about how to strengthen relationships. What will keep colleagues connected as organizations grow beyond 50, 500, or 5,000? Building and strengthening relationships, the conduits of culture. The answer is rituals.

THE IMPORTANCE OF RITUALS

A *ritual* is a recurring group activity designed to build and strengthen relationships. People organize rituals among friends (poker night) and family (Thanksgiving dinner) because they are moments to connect and share. And it feels good. Quality time spent together means stronger bonds. Similarly, companies have an opportunity to foster purposeful connections through rituals to counteract the cultural challenges of rapid growth. Without relationships the behaviors leaders want don't spread, and substitute cultures they may not like fill in. Just like they did with data analytics in the first decade of the twenty-first century, forward-thinking executives need to begin to turn a serious eye toward rituals and invest in strengthening the connective tissue of their organizations as they grow.

Rituals have two defining characteristics. The first characteristic is who leads: some are controlled from the top and others are employee-driven. The second characteristic is size: a ritual can be a small get-together for two, or one large enough to involve the entire company. Altogether, these characteristics result in four types of rituals: *explicit big group rituals, explicit small group rituals, emergent big group rituals,* and *emergent small group rituals.* No matter the category the only requirement is that it provides an opportunity to create or strengthen a relationship. That said, each one has its own strengths and challenges.

THE FOUR TYPES OF RITUALS

1. Explicit Big Group Rituals

Explicit big group rituals are those organized by the company and that reach at least the majority of the employees. Although a ritual at the intersection of explicit and big might have you recalling the last office holiday party you attended, there are many ways to strengthen relationships companywide. Let's think outside the punchbowl. Every summer, the San Francisco office of global design agency Landor Associates throws a festive picnic somewhere in the Bay Area. I had a chance to attend one of these when I interned during my senior year of design school. The entire SF office packed into a luxury bus to spend the day at a winery in Napa. This type of all-fun, no-work offsite goes a long way toward crossing typical office barriers as new relationships are created that transcend tenure and title.

Explicit rituals are organized and run by the company.

Infrequent budget busters aren't the only option, though. At the headquarters of Zappos in Las Vegas, a small riser in the cafeteria is staged with a stool and speakers for impromptu open mic lunches. While not every one of Zappos's 1,500 employees will hear that acoustic rendition of Radiohead's "Creep," the large hall ensures that quite a few Zapponians will learn that

BIG GROUP

EXPLICIT

EMERGENT

SMALL GROUP

RITUALS CAN BE LED FROM THE TOP OR BE

EMPLOYEE-DRIVEN; THEY CAN BE

COMPANYWIDE OR A GET-TOGETHER FOR TWO.

Ginny can sing. Rituals like these provide broad exposure and opportunities to learn about others in new ways. Not that you needed another reason to head out for some karaoke.

RITUAL CHECKLIST:
EXPLICIT BIG GROUPS

Does it facilitate new connections?
Successful big group rituals help employees meet and strengthen relationships with people from outside their typical social circle.

Is it consistent?
If the ritual is a hit, commit to hosting it regularly. Once is not enough; make sure employees get regular opportunities to meet and reconnect with colleagues.

Is it budgeted for?
Large-scale rituals tend to require a significant investment. Earmark some money so yours won't get left out during budgeting.

Is it inclusive?
When creating a large or companywide activity, consider every employee's needs so that everyone feels they can participate.

2. Explicit Small Group Rituals

Relationships can be built on a smaller scale, of course. A company-sponsored sports team or the "new hire coffee with the CEO" are classics in this category; they are terrific ways to connect those of different departments and rank.

At the digital publishing platform Medium.com, team meetings start with a check-in round, where people share a quick update about themselves. Jen Dennard, former People Ops team member at Medium, explains that these personal reports help people get to know one another and understand where their head is that day. "They may share what is going on in their work or personal lives; how they really, really need that cup of coffee they're holding; or how they ran into an old friend on the way to work today, so they're feeling extra jazzed about life." These personal updates have a larger, companywide effect: they bring a fruitful kind of vulnerability into Medium's daily routine.

"It's always tempting to just say 'I'm good,' but by sharing personal updates, each individual is practicing a moment of vulnerability," Jen shares. The updates allow each member of the group to have a deeper understanding for others during and after the meeting. These moments of connection nurture the culture of awareness and empathy that pervades Medium.

Finally, the check-ins also help make the meetings more inclusive. When an individual speaks at the beginning of the meeting, they are more likely to do so again. Jen says they've seen this effect most visibly with new hires. After speaking in their very first meeting, they feel more comfortable speaking up in general. Sounds like a win-win-win-win.

Like check-in rounds, most well-designed rituals foster a culture of awareness and empathy in addition to building relationships. Of course, relationships aren't all fun, so neither are rituals.

Jason Wisdom, cofounder of The Design Gym, shared a story about how the company addresses tensions and issues among the partners in a weekly meeting called "Uncomfortable Conversations." Running a growing business is hard. Throw in personal and family life, and there's no avoiding missed opportunities and challenging missteps.

In their weekly discussion, the partners gather to talk about personal anxieties, frustrations with each other, and frustrations with themselves. Jason says he's not only learned a lot about himself and his partners, but about the process as well. "In the same way that the business world draws a great deal of inspiration from design, I've found when trying to build a strong organizational culture there's a lot to be learned from relationship counselors. For example, a common way to present feedback to a partner or spouse is by saying: 'When you do (x behavior), it makes me feel (y feeling).' This phrase works because it's much more focused on acknowledging behaviors and personal emotions then assigning blame."

The benefit doesn't stop at the agency's front door either. At The Design Gym they often joke that their work is much more Dr. Phil than designer. Jason reports that through their Uncomfortable Conversations they have "developed the ability to help our clients better understand their own internal dynamics because we are constantly working on ourselves, and our own culture, especially when it's not comfortable."

When you are ready to create your own explicit small group rituals, look for opportunities to attract small groups that are open to new ideas and new people. (Getting everyone together to learn the new time tracking system doesn't count.)

RITUAL CHECKLIST:
EXPLICIT SMALL GROUPS

Is it understood? New rituals like meeting check-ins might seem weird at first—a change in process always is. The first time the ritual is introduced, share why it's important and what it looks like when it is done well.

Is it supported? Consider setting aside a little cash to keep the ritual alive. If the ritual is working, the return will be well worth the investment.

Is it a priority? As days get busy, rituals are easy to skip. Don't. Make these relationship strengtheners a priority.

3. Emergent Small Group Rituals

Emergent rituals are those that happen without management instigation. This category contains those small group behaviors that bloom organically: the regular lunch or the afternoon coffee. One of the most valuable attributes of emergent rituals is that they are authentic to the culture. Groups of twos and threes are a common size at first, but it doesn't mean they can't grow.

When a small group of employees at financial services start-up Credit Karma found they each played music they started a band. Leadership had the insight to support the endeavor and allow the group to play on company time. They even set aside a small office in which to rehearse and store their instruments. While executives could have easily pegged this as a waste of time, they encouraged this get-together, understanding that it brought a little more joy and connection into the company—things even the most successful FinTech company can't buy.

The challenge with emergent small group rituals is that by their very nature they are limited. Friends gather with those they know. Management should allow and even encourage teams to expand their circle and invite others to join them for coffee, to rock out, or bond over a yummy treat. This is exactly what teammates over at the growing Bay Area corporate catering company Zesty did when they formed Cheese Club.

Emergent rituals start organically without management instigation.

One afternoon an inspired Zesty manager set up an impromptu cheese tasting in the kitchen after stopping by Whole Foods. He invited a few colleagues to take part in sampling some soft triple cream, a hard Pecorino, and a local raw sheep's milk from Mendocino County, California. The tasting became a regular occurrence when foodies from across the company heard about it. Cheese Club became a culturally accurate way for zesties to bridge cubicles by bonding over cubes. And it started because someone was honestly just passionate about cheese. He didn't ask for permission or wait to schedule it. He just decided to do it. Leaders must be on the lookout for naturally occurring rituals like Cheese Club and do everything they can to support them.

RITUAL CHECKLIST:
EMERGENT SMALL GROUPS

Does it exist? Listen closely to see if you can identify these otherwise invisible rituals.

Can you help? Once identified, ask the group if there is anything you can do to provide support? "No" is a perfectly fine response.

Is it scalable? Are there ways to grow the ritual so others can participate? Look for opportunities, but don't force it.

Is it inclusive? Consider how to make small get-togethers available and welcoming to others.

4. Emergent Big Group Rituals

The gold standard of all these is the emergent big group ritual. Their scale enables the greatest cross-sampling of people and because they arise organically from people within the company they are more likely to be culturally relevant. Bonus: emergent big group rituals tend to be less expensive than the explicit big group rituals, but just as effective.

I love the story that comes from Northrop Grumman, an American global aerospace technology company. One of the engineers had a day-at-a-time Jeopardy calendar that he'd share with his friend nearby. It grew as the regular questions provided everyone within earshot a quick opportunity to engage in a playful morning ritual. What began between two cubicle mates evolved into a once-a-week trivia tournament that drew more and more employees. So many, in fact, that the festivities had to be moved into the common space to accommodate everyone interested.

To this day a sizeable gaggle of engineers come together and pool their smarts every Friday, tallying up their collective points over the entire year. Lighthearted rituals foster and strengthen relationships easily and naturally. Just like day-at-a-time Jeopardy between two coworkers grew to a weekly intradepartmental spectacle, look for emergent small-group rituals that can grow into the emergent big-group quadrant.

Champagne Friday is another great example of an emergent ritual at scale. This one developed at Journey CX, an innovation consulting firm out of Toronto. At the end of each week everyone comes together over a bottle of bubbly to celebrate small wins, share what has brought them joy, and recognize one another.

But this ritual is not just another happy hour. Taking a moment to acknowledge their work and each other is particularly important for the firm because their team has tendencies toward finding and focusing on problems. Journey CX's projects are often about creating long-term change, the results of which are hard to appreciate on a day-to-day basis. "Champagne Friday is an important reminder for us to celebrate wins big and small along the way and take pride in our progress," says cofounder Jessica Fan. This ritual is both a relationship builder and a buoy to keep their employees positive, motivated, and energized along the way. Santé!

Who better than your Culture All-Stars to help surface emergent rituals? They hold a unique position that might allow them to be a conduit between an organically occurring meetup and leadership. Ask your Culture All-Stars to listen for small get-togethers that could be great relationship builders if repeated or increased in size. They might also be the best people to find out more: Would the get-together benefit from a little bit of funding, a space for gathering, or more awareness?

RITUAL CHECKLIST:
EMERGENT BIG GROUPS

Who is a suitable leader? Look for a charismatic employee whom people naturally follow and trust.

Where is the opportunity? First look for emergent small-group rituals that might grow. Other opportunities might include working with an employee to support his or her passion project in which others can join.

What support does it need? Be willing to provide money, time, and space for these to grow, but have the restraint not to interfere.

Is it inclusive? When creating a large or companywide activity, consider every employee's needs so that everyone feels he or she can participate.

THE CHALLENGES OF CREATING RITUALS

Learning about great rituals from peers at other companies is a terrific way to bring new ideas back into your organization. But don't cut and paste without considering if they align with your company's values and culture.

I'm not talking about anything that breaks company policy. That's an HR issue. I mean rituals that encourage behaviors that might not align with your culture. If a company value is "do no harm" but a few members of the accounting department head to the shooting range every few weeks, is that value misaligned? I could never say definitively—that the decision should be left to people on the inside who understand the culture. Moments like these are great opportunities to remember to stay connected to purpose and values—they are your guides. Whatever choice is ultimately made, when it comes to what's right or wrong in a culture, being self-aware and asking questions are the most important parts.

THE WRONG SIDE OF RITUALS

Beyond those that aren't a good fit, managers must be aware of *unhealthy rituals*. Unlike any ill-conceived explicit or large-scale ritual, which will hopefully be caught before it is launched because of it's visibility, the small emergent variety will be the most problematic. Not only are they hard to spot, if they are self-organized between a few friends, the line between what is or is not a company ritual can be hard to define.

When it comes to spotting the unhealthy rituals, peers or leaders can only act on what they know. But not knowing doesn't absolve them of responsibility; legally speaking, managers are responsible even if they weren't there. This is another reason to keep an ear out for rituals that fly under the radar. Because of the liability, when an unhealthy ritual *is* identified, leaders need to quickly make it clear to the employees involved why it doesn't fit with the company culture, and then ask the employees to correct or replace the unhealthy ritual with a new, more appropriate one.

Another challenge with a ritual identified as unhealthy is that individuals may feel that what they are doing is not a company activity and therefore not part of the company's responsibility. This is a difficult place to be, and overstepping will seed distrust. Every situation is different, so proceed with caution.

A GREAT RITUAL

is authentic

fosters new relationships

is recurring

is supported by the company

might scale

is made a priority

has a "why" that is understood

There is no foolproof method to determine if an unhealthy ritual is a company issue, but here are some guidelines that may help:

- Is it on company property?
- Does it involve only employees, or are members of the public free to come and go?
- Is it on company time?
- Does it use company equipment?
- Will there be repercussions if someone chooses not to attend?
- Is it organized or encouraged by anyone in a managerial capacity?

It is hard to say what to do if the ritual involving employees is not within the control of the company. There's no doubt that even if it is off-hours and off campus, it has an impact on the company culture on some level.

People want to connect with one another, and if employees can't do so through department- or company-hosted rituals, they will fill that vacuum themselves. And what they end up with may not be the most authentic to the culture or inclusive of all employees. When rituals are thoughtfully designed, leaders support the evolution of the culture they want and set the tone for what it means to casually show up in a productive way. Ensure that the company happy hour on Friday afternoon includes nonalcoholic drinks. Or better yet, change the get-together to a Wednesday afternoon brown-bag lunch, when everyone can get outside for a little walk and some fresh air. By modeling these positive behaviors, employees have guidance for all rituals whether on company time or not.

CREATING INCLUSIVE RITUALS

More than any other component, rituals can exclude people. If your team grabs a beer after work, how will that make a colleague who doesn't drink feel? What about parents who need to pick up their kids—do they have to miss out on the bonding? This incidental exclusion can be the dark side of diverse work teams. If not every employee is a twenty-something white male, beer pong may not feel like the most welcoming event.

I'm not saying you can't grab a drink; it's not an either-or scenario. If there are more opportunities for all members to participate in, then it's fine to head to the beer garden from time to time. It's when the 5 p.m. drink becomes the primary form of bonding that problems arise.

Time of event or type of drink served aren't the only potentially exclusionary elements of ritual. Consider gender and communication: it is quickly becoming the norm to inquire about a person's preferred pronoun. Is it he/him, she/her, or they/them? Age and ability are two other important ones to consider. Is an older colleague less likely to participate in an aggressive physical activity? Will a person with a disability feel he or she can't contribute?

Employee resource groups (ERGs) are emerging as important tools in the movement to increase diversity and inclusion in organizations. They are also great rituals. A word of caution— ERGs *too* can be exclusive. Be clear that the women's leadership group is *about* women's leadership, not solely for women leaders. Encourage each woman to bring a man to increase ally-ship.[5] The same goes for any other ERG. The South Asian ERG is not just for South Asians; it's *about* South Asians. The black women's ERG is not just for black women; it's *about* black women.

There are many pieces to consider when it comes to creating inclusivity, but the most important consideration is making sure you know your colleagues. Ask people what they think about certain ideas, when they have dietary restrictions, or how they celebrate religious holidays; this may go a long way to making sure they feel included.

SCALING AND CULTURE TAXONOMIES

As powerful as rituals are, don't expect all parts of the organization to have the *exact* same culture. Variation is perfectly fine across divisions, offices, and regions. The key is to define what does and doesn't change across these populations. For example, a recognition program in Hamburg is going to be very different from one in El Paso. That's okay. The expression of culture, recognition, rituals, cues, and even some behaviors should change. What shouldn't change is the organization's purpose and values. How different can cultures be within a single organization? The rule of thumb is the less contact between individuals within two populations the less similar the culture. Physical distance is the largest contributing factor, but in the future, may play a less important role as digital tools bring regions closer together.

ALWAYS THE SAME	MAY BE THE SAME	RARELY THE SAME
Purpose Values	Behaviors	Recognition Rituals Cues

In geographically distributed organizations, the components of culture won't always look the same.

Rituals Quick-Start

Strengthen your organization's culture synapses by identifying which relationship-building rituals already exist and which need to be created.

HOW WILL EMPLOYEES BUILD AND STRENGTHEN RELATIONSHIPS?

Identify and Improve Existing Rituals

Rituals are key for high-growth organizations, but every company should put energy into helping employees build and strengthen relationships. This exercise will help you identify what rituals already exist, and create new ones.

Recruit two or three well-liked, but non-leadership employees to help. Bring them together to help you identify any rituals that already exist at your organization. The rituals can be of any size, from companywide to a small department get-together. Discuss which rituals work and what can be improved.

For any quadrant that doesn't have a ritual, use the examples in the chapter to inspire you to imagine new ones for your organization. What are other companies doing that, if adapted to your company, might work? Don't forget to test each idea against the Ritual Checklist questions to determine if it can be improved.

WHY YOU'RE DOING THIS
To help leaders understand the importance of rituals, and how to design them, particularly during times of growth.

HOW YOU'LL DO IT
A small-group working session.

WHO SHOULD PARTICIPATE
2 to 3 well-liked employees.

WHERE IT SHOULD HAPPEN
Anywhere with lots of wall space and room to work.

WHAT YOU'LL NEED
A few examples of rituals, pens and markers, a collaborative space like a whiteboard, a few standard-sized Post-it pads, and a set of worksheets for each participant including a blank rituals matrix.

HOW LONG YOU'LL NEED
2 hours.

Download this exercise to work on with your team at **greatmondays.com**

INSTRUCTIONS

1. With your two or three design confidants, walk through the rituals matrix a quadrant at a time and discuss if the organization, or any team within the company, performs rituals in that category. On the worksheet that follows, write down each ritual in the appropriate space provided.
   Time: 30 minutes

2. For each listed, talk about what works and what could be improved.
   Time: 20 minutes

3. For each quadrant invent one new ritual. Consider what you might need to create it. Who would need to be involved and what resources would it require? Write those answers down.
   Time: 30 minutes

4. On the third worksheet, evaluate each existing and new ritual against the quadrant's Rituals Checklist. Make a note of the number of "no" answers and any actions you might need to turn a "no" into a "yes."
   Time: 20 minutes

5. Using the questions decide which rituals will be most effective. Write those on a new sheet. These are the rituals you should further support or start implementing immediately.
   Time: 20 minutes

WHAT RITUALS DOES YOUR COMPANY ALREADY HAVE?

QUADRANT **1**	existing rituals	what works / what doesn't
explicit big group		

Write a new ritual for quadrant 1.

QUADRANT **2**	existing rituals	what works / what doesn't
emergent big group		

Write a new ritual for quadrant 2.

WHAT RITUALS DOES YOUR COMPANY ALREADY HAVE?

QUADRANT 3	existing rituals	what works / what doesn't
emergent small group		

Write a new ritual for quadrant 3.

QUADRANT 4	existing rituals	what works / what doesn't
explicit small group		

Write a new ritual for quadrant 4.

HOW DOES EACH RITUAL ANSWER IT'S KEY QUESTIONS?

QUADRANT 1	explicit big group
Ritual:	
Does it facilitate new connections?	
Is it consistent?	
Is it budgeted for?	
Is it inclusive?	

QUADRANT 2	emergent big group
Ritual:	
Is it understood?	
Is it supported?	
Is it a priority?	

QUADRANT 4	explicit small group
Ritual:	
Who is a suitable leader?	
Where is the opportunity	
What support does it need?	
Is it inclusive?	

QUADRANT 3	emergent small group
Ritual:	
Does it already exist?	
Can you help?	
Is it scalable?	
Is it inclusive?	

I have a lot of objects
in my space; little
things, reminders,
memories.

—Marc Newson

CHAPTER 7

Cues

The tedium of work can wear down even the most buoyant employee. The persistent punch list of emails, meetings, and budgets can make it hard to stay inspired. While leaders can't wish away the daily tasks that are connected to work, by wielding the right tools they *can* help teams stay inspired in the face of the day-to-day.

What are we doing? Why am I here? These questions are about the future—what we strive to do and become. Answers to questions like these, big and small, give work meaning and help us realign and become re-inspired. Without cues, even the most compelling vision of the future will eventually drown in more pressing problems. Work gets in the way. We get distracted. Enter *cues*, which are the physical and behavioral reminders that help employees, managers, and leaders stay connected to the future.

Without cues, even the most compelling vision of the future will eventually drown in more pressing problems.

Most companies already have a few cues in place, even if they don't realize it. Wall-sized mission statements are a common feature at headquarters the world over. These inspiration billboards are an easy way to make an organization's aspirations visible. It helps employees remember why they joined the company in the first place. But keeping employees connected to the bigger picture will take more than colorful decals; it will require a system of cues.

WHAT MAKES A CUE

I think about cues according to two factors. The first is whether the cue is a thing or an action, physical or behavioral. *Physical cues* can be seen, touched, or heard; examples include printed signs, digital messages, and conference room names for reminding people about goals. *Behavioral cues* are activities taken by leaders and peers; examples include the retelling of the corporate origin story to provide context, weekly one-on-ones that demonstrate the importance of growth and mentorship, and executives modeling work-life

Cues
The physical and behavioral reminders that help employees, managers, and leaders stay connected to the future.

balance by making sure people know they are actually taking time off and not "working from home."

The second factor is how *aspirational* a cue is. On one end are those *way* in the future. These cues help everyone remember the ultimate goal of the organization—its *purpose*. On the other end of the spectrum are reminders of more immediate aspirations and behaviors .

Immediate cues, those with the smallest gap between what is and what should be, tend to be tactical and reinforce values and working styles. A company that values a creative, iterative working style might supply Sharpies, abundant work surfaces, and post-its on every desk.

Immediate cues, those with
the smallest gap between
what is and what should
be, tend to be tactical
and reinforce values and
working styles.

In between the two extremes sit reminders about a near-term vision for the organization—say, where leaders hope to be in 12 to 24 months. These cues might help a team improve the way they work with difficult clients, or help a business unit achieve a certain level of success.

Mapping these two sets of factors on axes reveal four categories of cues every organization should consider including in their work lives. They are *physical immediate cues, behavioral immediate cues, behavioral aspirational cues,* and *physical aspirational cues.*

ASPIRATIONAL

PHYSICAL

BEHAVIORAL

IMMEDIATE

CUES REMIND PEOPLE ABOUT THE FUTURE

THEY ARE WORKING TOWARD.

1. Physical Immediate Cues

Cues in this quadrant are the most practical. They are tangible reminders of behaviors that can help everyone involved achieve a more successful, productive, and fulfilling work life. Dave Gray, founder of strategic-design consultancy XPLANE, took the traits that he wanted every employee and client to embody—characteristics like transparent communicators, goal visualizers, and flat managers—and drew them out on what he calls a *culture map*. Dave says one of the reasons he likes the map so much is because "it is a representation of the truth we are shooting for, and it's becoming more true every day."

It's worth noting that everyone at XPLANE believes in graphic tools because visualizing strategies is what they do for their clients. But even if you aren't a sketch artist, don't worry. There are plenty of ways to create your own physical immediate cues. Why not change "employee of the month" to "customer of the month"? Anyone not on the front lines could use a little help staying connected to the customer so they can remember the *who* behind the *why* of work. Want to encourage a culture of learning? Invest in a lending library program, physically in offices and digitally through Amazon.

Speaking of which, digital also falls into this quadrant. At Great Mondays we love Slack, and one of our channels is called #skill-up. Its very presence helps our team remember to share ideas, articles, and conferences in service of self-improvement.

A word of warning: while tremendously useful in fostering communication and a terrific opportunity for the deployment of cues, internal chat tools can be a distraction. Even Cal Henderson, the cofounder of Slack, knows it. I adore the approach he takes to manage all the noise and keep things from going too far astray; it's called the "polite raccoon."

Conversations on the platform inside of Slack include fun banter, but when it gets too much for one channel or the topic is no longer relevant to everyone else on that channel employees throw down a custom raccoon emoji, which means "take this conversation somewhere else." Everyone benefits from less message noise, and no one takes the nudge in the wrong way. Make sure physical and digital immediate cues are reminders of what we aspire to do today, but don't get in the way of doing it.

CUES CHECKLIST:
PHYSICAL IMMEDIATE CUES

Is it connected to an achievable action?	Cues in this quadrant should be reminders of choices that an individual or team can start to make immediately.
Does it stand on its own?	A physical cue may not always be accompanied by someone who can explain it. Design the cue to be understood in the moment.
Is it appropriate for the company culture?	Will employees feel it is authentic? Does it seem like something your company would do?

2. Behavioral Immediate Cues

Behaviors, too, can help shift an element of office life. For example, to solve the epidemic of meeting overload I've seen more than a few organizations proclaim one day meeting-free. Whether communicated by setting out-of-office emails, blocking off the company calendar, or setting your status to "do not disturb," on the specified day there is nothing but heads-down work.

Anyone in a leadership position has the right to call out choices that are outside the lines. Doing it across the organization, at an all-hands meeting or in an all-company email, sends a powerful message about what is and what is not acceptable.

I am a member of a Jewish community in San Francisco called the Kitchen. I go to pray, celebrate holidays with my family, and also help them with design and culture projects. During weekend Shabbat services, Rabbi Noa Kushner routinely makes it clear that clapping to show appreciation for someone isn't allowed. "This isn't a show. If you'd like to show praise yell 'Yasher Koach,' which means good job in Hebrew." You bet the community learned quickly the norms the rabbi is enforcing. I made that mistake exactly once.

No-Meeting Mondays and no clapping in services have very specific implications, but these kinds of cues can be used more broadly to great effect as well. Design and innovation consultancy Veryday had been working out of a converted church in a suburb of Stockholm for decades. How were they going to bring years of a unique Swedish-based culture to their new office in downtown Manhattan? Rikki Goldenberg, associate director of Project Management at Veryday, observes that "without the physical artifacts . . . it's up to the people." And so, with no charming church windows to remind American employees of its Swedish history, a regular behavioral cue fills that gap.

At 3 p.m. local time, across their offices, the teams break for Fika, the Swedish tradition of the afternoon coffee break. In Sweden, this universal social institution is about taking time to socialize with one's work colleagues. But by importing this behavior to New York City it takes on an additional layer of meaning. One can imagine that even new interns will quickly understand that Veryday's Swedish origin includes valuing the time to connect with others. Don't forget the biscuits.

CUES CHECKLIST:
BEHAVIORAL IMMEDIATE CUES

Is it connected to a quickly achievable action?	These cues should inspire behavior or goals that can be achieved in 18 months or less.
Does it strengthen relationships?	This cue might also be a ritual. Two for one culture tool. Sweet!
Can it spread?	Cues in this category are expressed through actions. If others can do it too, all the better.
Is it appropriate for the company culture?	Will employees feel it's authentic? Does it seem like something your company would do?

THE LINE BETWEEN RITUALS AND CUES

Behavioral cues can often also be rituals. Fika is a good example of a cue that builds relationships. Which of your rituals can also become a cue? Are there any behavioral cues that could also build new connections across your organization?

3. Behavioral Aspirational Cues

Cues in the third quadrant are communicated through actions of peers and leaders. But here they are reminders of bigger ideas, changes that occur on longer timelines, and repeated choices that are more difficult to enact.

Able Health created a cue that reinforces the idea that employees are expected to participate in the evolution of their culture. This healthcare start-up has put their culture guide on GitHub, a popular site among developers. GitHub is a web-based tool that makes it easier for many users to work on the same code at the same time. Or, at least, usually it's code. It turns out GitHub can be used with any kind of document.

Because Able Health's culture guide is on GitHub, they can make it public, updates can be suggested and approved, new versions can be created, or even used to create something different, which is exactly what's happened. Some of Able Health's clients have adapted it as their own culture guide. The genius of this approach? Able Health's team of tech-savvy folks understand the implication of this document being hosted here. They understand any document on GitHub isn't the outcome of some executive process, but the starting point for building something important together. For Able Health, the medium *is* the message and the platform *is* the cue.

A lot of companies are committing to "giving back" these days. They are contributing money, volunteering hours, and offering more help to their communities. These efforts can make for great cues. Salesforce is one of those enterprises that has invested a ton into philanthropy. Their approach is called the 1-1-1 philanthropic model (pronounced one to one to one) and has been around since 1999. The salesforce.org website says their purpose is to "leverage our technology, people, and resources to improve communities throughout the world." The program has had an impressive record of giving: over $168 million in grants, 2.3 million hours of service, and donations of their products to more than 32,000 nonprofits and educational institutions. When you are hired by Salesforce, your first day of work is spent volunteering. Many companies believe in volunteering, but the message this cue sends is that at Salesforce, it's central to what they do. This behavioral cue impresses this message upon its workforce on day one. Now that's a great cue.

Culture All-Stars are walking cues. How might you create opportunities for more employees to interact with them outside their teams? Is there a chance for them to share a great culture moment with the entire company? What about sending an email about a great win the company just scored? Your Culture All-Stars are one of your best assets. Use them well.

CUES CHECKLIST:
BEHAVIORAL ASPIRATIONAL CUES

Is it connected to a larger goal?

Aspirational cues should keep people connected to actions or ideals that are farther out on the timeline—anything from 18 months on.

Does everyone experience it?

The more aspirational the cue the more likely the ideal or goal is relevant to the entire company. In its current form, how many people does the cue reach?

Can it spread?

Cues in this category are expressed through actions—if others can do it too, all the better.

Does it strengthen relationships?

Your cue might also be a ritual. Go with it.

Is it appropriate for the company culture?

Will employees feel it's authentic? Does it seem like something your company would do?

4. Physical Aspirational Cues

We already discussed the ubiquitous mission statement on the wall, but what are other markers of bigger ideas that can inspire visually? Proposition Chicken, a quirky San Francisco Bay Area quick-serve restaurant, plucked language from their employee handbook turning their purpose into signage.

Thanks to owner Ari Feingold's diligent onboarding efforts, everyone on the staff of Proposition Chicken knows why the restaurant exists: "To serve the best damn chicken (and yummy people, too)." When they opened a new storefront in Oakland, it was a bold but on-brand choice to paint "This way to the best damn chicken" above the rear entrance. And it is. If you are ever in the Bay Area, stop by for the fried chicken sandwich.

Even if you don't have a storefront, there are other ways to build aspiration into office infrastructure. A relatively easy one that can have companywide impact is conference room names.

If you were to step into the San Francisco office of innovation consultancy Frog, you would immediately see an atrium surrounded by frosted-glass enclosed conference rooms. Each room's door is inscribed with a name that tells part of the organization's story.

On the left a door leading to the first room reads "Founder's Club," under which a sentence describes how designer Hartmut Esslinger started Frog in Germany's Black Forest region. Walk a few steps farther and the next room, "Passport," relays the firm's aspirations: the name is accompanied by the sentence describing that Frog "strives to move markets and change minds in all four corners of the world." This thoughtful suite of cues ensures that even casual visitors learn about the firm's humble beginnings, and not-so-humble ambitions.

Another powerful physical aspirational cue comes from the gaming behemoth Zynga. Anyone who has ever walked in the doors to their headquarters near San Francisco's Design Center knows this company is all about play. Live video feeds of gamers from around the world are shown in the lobby on an enormous floor-to-ceiling matrix of monitors. You can bet that even the janitorial staff understands what the company does and why.

CUES CHECKLIST:
PHYSICAL ASPIRATIONAL CUES

Is it connected to a larger goal?	Aspirational cues should keep people connected to actions or ideals that are farther out on the timeline—anything from 18 months on.
How many people does it reach?	The more aspirational the cues are the more likely the ideal or goal is relevant to the entire company. In its current form, how many people does it reach?
Will it scale?	Can it be changed or amplified to increase its exposure?
Does it stand on its own?	A physical cue may not always be accompanied by someone who can explain it. Design the cue to be understood in the moment.
Is it appropriate for the company culture?	Will employees feel it's authentic? Does it seem like something your company would do?

MORE CUES FOR INSPIRATION

Basic Cues

- Include the organization's purpose in email footers. It's easy to do and the volume of email bouncing around insures no one will likely forget the organization's purpose.
- Slack gives the ability to change the messages users see when the app starts. Update the message every few months to communicate what the company is trying to achieve. Keep it short though—anything longer than a sentence will probably be ignored.

Intermediate Cues

- Here at Great Mondays we send our friends, clients, and colleagues a mug that says TGIM. "Thank God It's Monday" is a great way to share the optimism we promote, and the goal to make work so meaningful that even Mondays can be great. (Want one? Greatmondays.com has my contact info. Send me a note and I'll put one in the mail for you.)
- Start staff meetings with a success story. A quick retelling of how an individual or group achieved a goal is worth the two and a half minutes it takes to share. Expand the idea beyond just company wins—what are people or communities outside of the company doing to support a purpose similar to yours?

Advanced Cues

- When paired with the right moment, physical symbols can have great meaning. A *token* can be defined as a memento or souvenir, but it can also refer to an item or idea that is a part representing the whole. Imagine creating an object that represents the commitment the company has made toward reaching its purpose and then give it to each new employee during onboarding. The item can be a way to access the enthusiasm the employee felt when joining the company, and a reminder of the company's bigger goal. But make sure it's compelling and something that employees want to keep around. It won't do anyone any good if it is stashed in a drawer at home.

  Consider anything from a trinket that can be kept *on* a desk, to a bracelet or pin, to a hardbound book that documents the company's culture. But don't stop at onboarding. What if you created a system of patches presented at anniversaries or for achievements? A ceremony to present these tokens of accomplishments in service of the company purpose can serve as a great way to keep reminding people why they come to work.

CUES COME IN ALL FLAVORS

A system of well-designed cues can help employees float above banal tasks and stay connected to a compelling vision of the future, near and far. But it will take a varied mix, regularly deployed, to be truly effective.

Where should you start? That depends on your sphere of influence. Cues can and should be designed at different scales—from department to companywide. The leader of a small eight-person group should think about how to keep each individual connected to the team's near-term aspirations. The VP of human resources should think about what tools are at her disposal to remind every employee of the company's purpose. Even individuals can set up their own cues. Simply writing a personal purpose statement, taking a photo of it, and setting it as his or her computer home screen can be a daily reminder of what the employee hopes to achieve this month, this year, or in life.

Keeping Track of Cues

Cues are everywhere. The trick is to be conscious of them. What job are the cues performing, and in which category do they sit? Begin by recording those cues that already exist in a Google Doc to share with your team. Ask others how they come across. Then consider how effective they are. Which cues can be improved? Are there cues waiting to be activated? Organizations should look for ways to gauge whether a cue is effective, and if it lasts over time. How often do employees encounter the cue in a month? How often does the cue come up in conversation? Do the employees understand what the cue is a reminder of?

Which cues are helpful to your team? Where could you do better? To find the ones that will be best for your business, it's going to take rigor, observation, and a little creativity. Let's get started.

Cues Quick-Start

Keep employees connected to the company's future by creating new physical and behavioral cues.

HOW WILL EMPLOYEES STAY CONNECTED TO THE FUTURE?

Design Your Company's Physical and Behavioral Cues

How will your employees remember why they come to work? Craft reminders large and small to help them stay connected, even when the pressures of deadlines and project plans threaten. When cues are embedded throughout the employee experience, these consistent physical, digital, and behavioral symbols can reenergize individuals and provide the lift they need to make it through difficult moments and inevitable long days.

WHY YOU'RE DOING THIS
To help leaders get started designing cues.

HOW YOU'LL DO IT
A small-group working session.

WHO SHOULD PARTICIPATE
2 to 3 creative employees who have been with the company over a year.

WHERE IT SHOULD HAPPEN
Anywhere with lots of wall space and room to work.

WHAT YOU'LL NEED
Your list of behaviors from Chapter 4, your company purpose statement, markers, Post-it Notes, whiteboards or wall space, and a set of worksheets for each participant.

HOW LONG YOU'LL NEED
2 hours.

Download this exercise to work on with your team at **greatmondays.com**

INSTRUCTIONS

1. With your creative partners, brainstorm a list of cues that will help employees remember the company's purpose. Start by listing at least five physical cues.
    HINT: *Don't worry if the ideas aren't great, just write them down. In the creative process, starting is often the hardest part.*
    Time: 15 minutes

2. Repeat step one, but this time write out at least five digital cues.
    Time: 15 minutes

3. Finally come up with at least five behaviors that leadership can model to keep employees inspired by the company purpose. Consider if there are any existing opportunities from which you can create a cue, either physical, digital, or behavioral.
    Time: 15 minutes

4. Once your group has at least 15 ideas, evaluate which are most likely to be successful by testing your ideas against the Cues Checklist.
    Time: 20 minutes

5. Take the three or four most promising ideas—those that best answered the questions from the Checklist—and create a list of what you will need to make them real. Set aside the rest but keep a record for inspiration the next time you need to create new cues.
    Time: 30 minutes

LIST CUES THAT ALIGN WITH YOUR COMPANY'S PURPOSE.

Write your purpose		
physical	digital	behavioral

EVALUATE YOUR BEST IDEAS AGAINST THE CUES CHECKLIST AND HOW APPROPRITE IT IS FOR YOUR CULTURE.

PHYSICAL AND DIGITAL ASPIRATIONAL CUES		
	CUE 1	**CUE 2**
Is it connected to a larger goal?		
How many people does it reach?		
Will it scale?		
Does it stand on its own?		
How appropriate for your culture?		

BEHAVIORAL ASPIRATIONAL CUES		
	CUE 3	**CUE 4**
Is it connected to a larger goal?		
Does everyone experience it?		
Does it strengthen relationships?		
Can it spread?		
How appropriate for your culture?		

CHAPTER 8

The Future of Culture

The only place to end is where we began. Business is changing faster than you think. Like a whiffle ball in the wind, businesses will continue to be knocked around by a volatile, uncertain, complex, and ambiguous world. New companies steal market share in the dead of night, as the creation and destruction of value moves further from a company's control, and customers exert the power of digital media.

The future of work is not some futurist's far-off prediction—it is now. I'm seeing some emerging trends that I'm willing to bet will become leading practices quickly. Let's start with a few of the closest futures and make our way out from there.

THE NEAR FUTURE

Goodbye Culture Fit; Hello Values Fit

You may have heard that *culture fit* is a challenging term. Busy recruiters and managers use the term as a shortcut to describe the kind of person they are looking to hire. The problem is that while it's easy to refer to "culture fit," it is never well-defined.

The term can be code for hiring people just like the rest of the employees. We tend to be drawn to people with similar life experiences and a similar worldview—it's reassuring and fun to be surrounded by people like us. That's fine for friendships, but it is problematic when it comes to hiring. Study after study reveals that diverse workplaces are the most attractive,[1] effective,[2] creative,[3] and successful.[4] Hiring like-minded individuals through culture fit leads to groupthink, and narrow conclusions, not to mention *un*-diversity. Instead, look for *values fit*—people who have complimentary working styles, motivations, and beliefs.

Welcoming individuals from different economic, geographic, or educational background is not easy. The shorthand we use to quickly connect and communicate with people from similar backgrounds no longer works. It takes some doing to get to know someone. But the initial effort will be well worth the productivity and engagement that comes from hiring people who hold the same beliefs about how the best work gets done.

Self-Driving Isn't Just for Cars

In this brave new world of shortening tenure (18 months in Silicon Valley, 24 months everywhere else), workers can no longer rely on one or two organizations to define their career.

It will be the explicit responsibility of people to create their own infrastructure to support themselves across roles, jobs, and years.

Mentors, coaches, skills training, and networking—the career-molding perks that once came with working for an organization for an extended period—are no longer viable. Today, the most successful individuals will have to take an active role in planning and designing their careers. And new strategies are being created all the time.

Building a personal brand was never something workers had to concern themselves with before. But now, it's essential to manage your reputation. According to Google, since 2004, search interest in the term "personal brand" has quadrupled, which isn't surprising. In today's work world, curating a career is critical. Anyone who wants to climb higher will need to build their own corporate ladder.

The Whole-Self Workplace

How will companies turn around the dismally low number of highly engaged employees? To be committed, people need to feel supported, and not just in their jobs. Gone are the days of leaving personal business at the door and putting on a positive face for an eight-hour shift.

Is someone going through a difficult situation at home? The best perk a company can offer is peers who can be there to listen—a social community of people who understand one another and can provide support if needed.

To baby boomers, it may seem like coddling, but giving people the space to have feelings and to be themselves at work is the new norm. A special shout-out to all the brave LGBTQ folks doing just that.

As leaders expect people to commit more to work, people are expecting more from their leaders. The environment that a Whole-Self Workplace provides helps everyone to be more present at work and to be committed to the company.

Gone will soon be the days when employees are discouraged from having feelings. An accomplished, engaged, and motivated workforce is made up of people who don't feel it's necessary to hide parts of themselves that in the past were considered unprofessional. It's okay to talk about your family life, good and bad. It should be okay to share emotions and events happening in your life. Your coworkers can also be your support network. "Have your feelings or they'll have you," goes the saying. The truth is no one ever really left anything at the door anyhow.

A New Path to Talent

The war for talent is escalating, but you don't have to fight that battle. Executives in highly competitive businesses operate on the premise that talent is a scarce resource. They tell their recruiters to use the same criteria to hunt for the same people as everyone else. For most organizations that's a losing proposition, and a waste of energy.

When specific skills are in demand, it is easy to think of talent as an absolute. It's not. Smart leaders already understand that the top candidate for one company may not be ideal for another.

To avoid flooding the market with generic job descriptions, business leaders will need to put in more work up front, coaching recruiters, and thinking through what *their* organization needs. Looking for great candidates that fit requires creativity. In her book *Powerful: Building a Culture of Freedom and Responsibility*, Patty McCord, former chief talent officer at Netflix, shares a story of finding a talented developer at a bank in Arizona. Someone on Patty's team found the Netflix-enhancing app that he had posted to his website. On paper he didn't seem like an obvious choice, but he turned out to be a great employee because he was going to get to work on what he loved.

What peers and competitors describe as "the best" may not necessarily be the best for you. Don't let high-pressure hiring goals force you to take shortcuts and a brute-force approach. By putting the time into unconventional thinking and recruiting you'll conserve cash, improve engagement, and experience lower turnover with talented candidates who are particularly well-suited for this role and this company.

THE MIDDLE FUTURE

Retention Is Dead: Long Live Work Cycles

Earlier in the book I proclaimed that a great culture would help companies keep employees. And that's true. But retention programs may soon not be worth the energy needed to run them.

Rapidly dropping tenure and increasing numbers of contractors have created a market force ripping employees from their desks. Continued escalation of those trends leads to a world that moves too fast for retention. It just doesn't make sense to spend six months hiring and onboarding someone who'll only stay for another year.

This future was foreshadowed in 2014 when LinkedIn cofounder Reid Hoffman made a case for "tours of duty" in his book, *The Alliance: Managing Talent in the Networked Age*. The central concept proposed a new social contract of work that would benefit both employer and employee. What if instead of working full-time for as long as one could stand it, we signed a shorter-term agreement that could be renewed if both the company and the contractor agreed. When I read this it landed for me like a ton of timesheets.

A change of this magnitude doesn't just happen. Futurist Paul Saffo once said, "Never mistake a clear view for a short distance."[5] A lot needs to shift inside an organization to make an idea like Reid's tours of duty possible.

Here are four key pieces every organization needs to start changing, even if they have no intention of eliminating full-time employment:

1. *Turn a "No" into an Advocate.* An organization with a solid pipeline always has more people walk away without an offer than the one person who gets it. Turn a "no" into a brand advocate by putting time and energy into designing a great candidate experience.

   Treat every person who comes to your company with respect and kindness, not just because it's the right thing to do—which it is—but because he or she might send you your next candidate. Or as the company evolves, this person might end up coming back to be a good fit in the future.

2. *Flip Your Onboarding.* Briefing new talent is a must-have in the employee life cycle, but the problem is that these processes often take too long and cover the wrong things. Sure policies and procedures are important, but do we need to spend days to review them? Why not flip your onboarding program?

Progressive educators use *the flipped classroom model,* where class time is reserved for "homework" and the responsibility of learning new material is done at home. Perhaps it's time for onboarding to be flipped.

Don't waste time teaching procedures and policies that can be learned individually online. Instead prioritize company culture and relationships. These human elements are typically left for employees to muddle through on their own, but they shouldn't be. When learned quickly, befriending the people who understand how the company works, and the culture behind it, will give employees what they need to succeed as they ramp up.

3. *Make Projects Modular.* If talent is at risk of leaving sooner rather than later, structure projects in a way that will ensure individuals can create the most value in a short amount of time. There are many ways to do it: operate in project sprints, create *tiger teams* to tackle one big challenge faster, or get great at running Agile project management.

These short, fast bursts of work create a sense of momentum, but also create a structure that helps minimize the disruption if (when) someone on the team leaves. Segmentation is a compelling way to begin to change work processes so that employee turnover no longer costs the company as much in time and money.

4. *Keep in Touch with Alumni.* Everyone will leave; it's a fact of the future. No longer are hard feelings necessary as more people get better at moving on. Don't think of them as having left the company, but as moving into a new role of

brand advocate and alumni. Your new and growing company diaspora can be a powerful cadre of advocates who may send you your next All-Star or customer.

At the end of the day, the biggest change may not be in processes but in attitudes. As shorter tenures become the norm, it will no longer be a secret that workers are already thinking about their next move while they start their current project. The question isn't if it'll happen, but when companies will embrace it.

Work-Life Balance? Ha! (or Here Comes Gen Z)

Like it or not, Gen Z is coming. Where millennials see a struggle to keep their "always-on" personal life away from their work world, Gen Z hardly notices. For the next generation now entering the workforce, there is no difference between work and life. There is no difference between their desk at home, a table at a coffee shop, and a conference room in an office.

The same goes for digital. There's no expectation that being somewhere in person is any less effective than being on video chat. The line between physical and digital has all but vanished for these folks, and that means business needs to make sure it's ready for this.

If you thought it was ridiculous when Marissa Mayer, former president and CEO of Yahoo!, banned nearly all remote work in 2013, just wait until executives attempt to enforce working hours as these digital natives enter the workforce. Any decrees will be met with a giant ¯_(ツ)_/¯ as they walk out the door.

This new labor force doesn't work like the rest of the world. They don't think twice about taking off two hours for errands or a bike ride during the day because of course they'll be online working at night. The term "working hours" has no meaning to them. For Gen Z, there's no need to hunt for a work-life balance. It's all mashed together all the time. Be aware, though. An even bigger change will accompany Gen Z: the blurring of the line between the inside and outside of companies.

THE FARTHER FUTURE

Communities, Not Customers

The ecosystem of business is changing and so are the players. In the not-so-distant future narrow terms like "employee" and "customer" will no longer suffice. Take Airbnb. Hosts aren't employees, but they do play the role of client services and inventory management. They aren't customers either, yet they are wooed by the company as if they were. In the eyes of the law they might be contractors, but the definition still falls short in meaning.

Businesses don't have employees and customers any longer; they have *communities* where value can be created in new ways and come from unexpected places. A savvy social media maven can have a more direct impact than any member in marketing. Paid or not, a single influencer can create interest in a product, service, or brand way beyond what a single customer ever could.

Roles are changing on the inside as well. It's not difficult to imagine a corporation expanding the responsibilities of employees and investing in training to help individuals become more effective brand advocates in person and online. What about alumni? If handled well, a former employee can and will want to contribute—buying products, telling others, or even by recommending the next hire. Inside and out, these people all contribute to the business, but some of the most important players in the system can't be controlled through paychecks and mandates.

As new players emerge, and old positions fade, it's hard to say how these extreme hybrid roles (if you can even call them that) evolve. What *is* evident is that business leaders must change how they see the world; they need to zoom out, so they can see more of *who* is connected to *what*. In the future, we won't be talking about companies trying to attract employees and sell to customers. The conversation will be about one community, inside and out, working together to achieve a single purpose. And when a business's control over these sometimes-paid roles is tentative at best, the best tool we have is culture.

In the future, the conversation will be about one community working together to achieve a single purpose.

Build Your External Community Culture

Designing company culture isn't enough anymore. Sophisticated brands will foster and design the culture of their external communities. It may not be as far-off in the future or as extraordinary as it sounds. The early precursor of this trend lays in the work done by community and social media managers as they listen to the world, support champions with status and rewards, and rush to soothe any disgruntled participants.

Outside of those roles, community culture design isn't a practice most companies have experience in. But there is a category of business that can teach other companies a thing or two: nonprofits. Because the proportion of staff of nonprofits to the people they serve is typically much smaller than that of other organizations, nonprofits can serve as a model for the next evolution of external culture management. In Chapter 7, I wrote about Rabbi Noa Kushner and The Kitchen. I bring it up again here because it is exactly the kind of organization engaging in community culture design.

The Kitchen was founded by Rabbi Kushner in 2012 as an experiment in creating a way for anyone who wants to "do Jewish" to come together. As a community member and consultant, I have had the opportunity to watch from a front-row seat the growth and operations of this novel religious institution. Since she started, Kushner has held a vision of a community of people who are uniquely Kitchen-y in the way they gather and engage with the institution and with one another. She builds programs, hires staff, and gives talks all in service of this vision. Until recently, neither she nor I realized that all along this approach had been designing the culture of the community.

QUESTIONS FOR BUILDING COMMUNITY CULTURE

1. What might be authentic ways to share our purpose outside our company?

2. How will our values inform our products and services?

3. What are examples of values-driven behaviors in our external community?

4. How can we recognize and reward our community?

5. What rituals can we help bring about so those on the outside can connect?

6. What will cues look like when designed for use outside the company walls?

Now that it is no longer in start-up mode, scaling The Kitchen in the right way is the focus. How will an organization like this bring on staff and clergy that can curate and amplify the culture? To that end Rabbi Kushner asked me to help her and the board identify and codify the values of the organization. In the end, the values we developed are guides for not just the staff, but for the hundreds of members. It has been a thrilling experience to see this work come to life, and I'm eager to see how it continues to evolve.

This can work for a community of a few hundred people, but what about a community in the tens of thousands? An external culture practice at city-size comes from Victoria Mitchell, the operations leader at Burning Man Project. Victoria's team is responsible for the annual evaluation, planning, mapping, communication, and on-site placement of approximately 1,500 camps and 55,000 people.

Globally there are about 100 employees at Burning Man Project, but most of the people Victoria works with are volunteers and community leaders. Victoria sees her job as part city planner and part culture cultivator. She and others at the organization think a lot about how to propagate the culture for which Burning Man Project is known. Not just for staff, but also across teams, volunteers, camps, and Burners who come together to create one of the largest cities in Nevada for a few weeks every year.

The culture is still a work in progress, and if there is a secret sauce the Burning Man Project is still working on it. However, there is a thread that has emerged as the organization has grown. As much as they need to continue the culture that the event is known for, they've learned autonomy is just as important. Individuals and camps want to act out their own unique version of the culture. In fact, some might say that's the point of the event. Victoria and her peers realize that success in community culture building will require a balance between the guidance of the organization and the expression of the community.

External culture building won't be easy. But in a future, where more people who aren't on the payroll play a role in the business, it will be necessary. You can't tell people who aren't paid by you to follow the rules—but with the right strategy and tools it is possible to influence the culture of external communities as much as internal communities. As the distinction of who is inside and outside of an organization gets harder to recognize, how might we use the six components of culture—Purpose, Values, Behaviors, Recognition, Rituals, and Cues—to create value for our communities and the company?

THE KEEL OF BUSINESS

Culture is the keel that gives business stability and lift, even when change blows from every direction. When people are part of an organization that provides inspiration, guidance, acknowledgment, and community they will do their best work no matter the circumstances. And I believe that with the right intention, and with the right tools, every company can make that happen.

I see a world in which every business leader, from manager to chief executive, considers culture design one of the most important jobs they can do. Why? Because in this world, culture is the only true sustainable business advantage.

From manufacturing furniture in the Bronx to developing apps in the Valley, how we define success will continue to change. But, what people need to do their best work never will.

Here's to creating a company culture that employees love,

NOTES

Introduction

1. https://www.glassdoor.com/research/studies/does-company
   -culture-pay-off-analyzing-stock-performance-of-best-places
   -to-work-companies/.

Chapter 1

1. http://www.refinery29.com/2016/02/103896/zenefits-sex-in
   -stairwells.
2. https://www.lifehacker.com.au/2016/02/inside-githubs
   -culture-war-thats-ripping-the-us2-billion-startup-apart/.
3. https://gizmodo.com/mark-zuckerberg-asks-racist-facebook
   -employees-to-stop-1761272768.
4. https://www.greatplacetowork.com/best-workplaces/100-best
   /2017.
5. https://medium.com/@MaiaJo/how-to-understand-the-roi-of
   -investing-in-people-b0049e006a84.
6. Schein, Edgar H. *Organizational Culture and Leadership* (The
   Jossey-Bass Business & Management Series), 5th ed. Hoboken,
   NJ: Wiley, 2016.
7. Stiehm, Judith Hicks. *The U.S. Army War College: Military Education in a Democracy.* Philadelphia: Temple University Press, 2002,
   p. 6.
8. https://www2.deloitte.com/us/en/pages/human-capital
   /articles/introduction-human-capital-trends.html.
9. https://hbr.org/2017/05/onboarding-isnt-enough.

10. http://blog.bersin.com/bersin-launches-new-recognition
    -research-a-hidden-secret-to-talent-management/.
11. "State of the American Workplace." 2017. https://news.gallup
    .com/reports/199961/7.aspx?utm_source=SOAW&utm
    _campaign=StateofAmericanWorkplace&utm_medium=
    2013SOAWreport.

Chapter 2

1. https://www.brainyquote.com/quotes/john_mackey_697678.
2. https://en.wikipedia.org/wiki/Friedman_doctrine.

Chapter 4

1. https://www.psychologytoday.com/us/articles/199911/were
   -all-copycats.

Chapter 6

1. https://en.wikipedia.org/wiki/Size_of_groups,_organizations,
   _and_communities#Intimate_communities.
2. Stambor, Zak. apa.org. (April 2006, Vol. 37, No. 4). Bonding
   over others' business. https://www.apa.org/monitor/apr06
   /bonding.aspx.
3. https://en.wikipedia.org/wiki/Robin_Dunbar2.
4. http://www.lifewithalacrity.com/.
5. http://www.guidetoallyship.com/.

Chapter 7

1. Salesforce.org.

Chapter 8

1. https://www.glassdoor.com/press/twothirds-people-diversity
   -important-deciding-work-glassdoor-survey-2/.
2. http://www.hult.edu/blog/benefits-challenges-cultural
   -diversity-workplace/.
3. https://hbr.org/2013/12/how-diversity-can-drive-innovation.

4. https://www.mckinsey.com/business-functions/organization
   /our-insights/is-there-a-payoff-from-top-team-diversity.
5. http://longnow.org/seminars/02008/jan/11/embracing
   -uncertainty-the-secret-to-effective-forecasting/.

INDEX

ABOUT THE AUTHOR

Josh Levine is an educator and designer on a mission to help organizations design a culture advantage. For over 15 years, he has worked closely with technology and social enterprise organizations, helping build culture-driven brands.

He is the principal of Great Mondays and cofounder of the nonprofit Culture LabX, where as executive director he has overseen its growth into an international community. Each year, tens of thousands of culture professionals attend Culture LabX events and engage in deep conversations about advancing and advocating for culture as a strategic advantage in business.

Josh is sought after for his inspiring and educational keynotes, and has spoken for numerous organizations including SXSW, Disrupt HR, and the Wellness Council of America. And because he just can't get enough, you will also find him sharing his ideas as an instructor in the groundbreaking MBA program in design at the California College of the Arts, as well as in articles featured in Forbes, Huffington Post, Fast Company, and the Design Management Journal—to name just a few.

Josh holds a BS in engineering psychology from Tufts University and BFA in design from the Academy of Art University.